Project Management Institute

CHOOSING APPROPRIATE PROJECT MANAGERS
MATCHING THEIR LEADERSHIP STYLE TO THE TYPE OF PROJECT

CHOOSING APPROPRIATE PROJECT MANAGERS
MATCHING THEIR LEADERSHIP STYLE TO THE TYPE OF PROJECT

Rodney Turner, PhD
Professor of Project Management
Graduate School of Management Lille

and

Ralf Müller, DBA
Umeå School of Business
Umeå University

ISBN 13: 978-1-933890-20-3
ISBN 10: 1-933890-20-7

Published by: Project Management Institute, Inc.
Four Campus Boulevard
Newtown Square, Pennsylvania 19073-3299 USA.
Phone: +610-356-4600
Fax: +610-356-4647
E-mail: pmihq@pmi.org
Internet: www.pmi.org

© 2006 Project Management Institute, Inc. All rights reserved.

"PMI", the PMI logo, "PMP", the PMP logo, "PMBOK", "Project Management Journal", "PM Network", and the PMI Today logo are registered marks of Project Management Institute, Inc. The Quarter Globe Design is a trademark of the Project Management Institute, Inc. For a comprehensive list of PMI marks, contact the PMI Legal Department.

PMI Publications welcomes corrections and comments on its books. Please feel free to send comments on typographical, formatting, or other errors. Simply make a copy of the relevant page of the book, mark the error, and send it to: Book Editor, PMI Publications, Four Campus Boulevard, Newtown Square, PA 19073-3299 USA.

PMI books are available at special quantity discounts to use as premiums and sales promotions, or for use in corporate training programs, as well as other educational programs. For more information, please write to Bookstore Administrator, PMI Publications, Four Campus Boulevard, Newtown Square, PA 19073-3299 USA, or e-mail: booksonline@pmi.org. Or contact your local bookstore.

Printed in the United States of America. No part of this work may be reproduced or transmitted in any form or by any means, electronic, manual, photocopying, recording, or by any information storage and retrieval system, without prior written permission of the publisher.

The paper used in this book complies with the Permanent Paper Standard issued by the National Information Standards Organization (Z39.48—1984).

10 9 8 7 6 5 4 3 2 1

Table of Contents

List of tables vii

List of figures ix

Executive summary xi

Chapter 1: Introduction 1
   The research project 2
   Structure of this report 3

Chapter 2: Leadership 5
   The schools of leadership 5
   The competency school of leadership 10
   Cultural behaviors of leaders 12
   Leadership styles and context 13
   Personality and team behaviors 16
   Conclusion 18

Chapter 3: Project Success 19
   Project success factors 19
   The project manager as a success factor 23
   Project success criteria 25
   The project management literature on project categorization 27

Chapter 4: Research Methodology 31
   Aims and approach 31
   Research model 31
   Interviews 34
   Web-based questionnaire 35
   Validation 36
   Project manager profiles 36

Chapter 5: Interviews 39
   Companies interviewed 39
   Types of projects 40
   Success criteria 42
   Criteria for selecting project managers 42
   Rating leadership competencies 43
   Summary 44

Chapter 6: Web-based Questionnaire 47
   Competences and competencies correlated to high-performing projects 47
   Validation 53

Chapter 7: Project Manager Profiles 63
   Profiles by application area 63
   Profiles by project complexity 65
   Profiles by project importance 67

  Profiles by contract type 69
  Profiles by life-cycle stage 71

Chapter 8: Recommendations and Conclusions 75
  Research questions and hypotheses 75
  Practical implications 76
  Theoretical implications 77
  Implications for the project management community 77

Appendix A: Author Contact Details 79

Appendix B: Fifteen Competency Dimensions of Leadership 81
  Emotional Competencies (EQ) 81
  Managerial Competencies, (MQ) 81
  Intellectual Competencies (IQ) 81

Appendix C: Project Categories 83

Appendix D: Interview Questions 85
  Nature of the company 85
  Project success 85
  Project manager's personality style and project type 85
  Selecting project managers 85
  Anything else 85

Appendix E: Interview Data 87
  Company information 87
  Nature of projects undertaken 87
  Project success 87
  Selecting project managers 87

Appendix F: Web-based Questionnaire 101
  (A) Project types 101
  (B) Project success 102
  (C) Demographics 103
  (D) Competencies 103

Appendix G: Web-based Questionnaire Data and Analysis 105
  Sample demographics 105
  Quantitative analysis of questionnaire data 107
  Validation 108
  Project manager on high-performing projects 109
  Individual profiles 112

References 113

Bibliography 117

List of Tables

2-1	The schools of leadership	6
2-2	Models of leadership style based on five parameters	7
2-3	Four styles of project leader (Turner 1999)	8
2-4	Leadership styles, project team types, and the project life cycle	9
2-5	Domains of emotional intelligence	10
2-6	Fifteen leadership competencies as suggested by Dulewicz and Higgs (2003), and the competency profiles of three leadership styles	11
2-7	Performance of different leadership styles on different types of change projects	12
2-8	Cultural dimensions of leadership after Hofstede (1991) and Trompenaars (1993)	13
2-9	Fourteen leadership functions according to Krech, Crutchfield, and Ballachey (1962)	14
2-10	Management style versus product portfolio and life-cycle	15
2-11	Dimensions of the multifactor leadership questionnaire (Bass, 1990)	15
2-12	The sixteen personality factors after Cattell, Eber, and Tatsuoka (1970)	16
2-13	Belbin's team roles and associated characteristics	17
2-14	Team roles identified by Margerison and McCann (1990)	17
3-1	Project success factors, after Andersen et al. (1987)	20
3-2	Project success factors after Morris (1988)	20
3-3	Project success factors after Baker, Murphy, and Fisher (1988)	21
3-4	Project success factors after Pinto and Slevin (1988)	21
3-5	Project success factors after Cooke-Davies (2001)	23
3-6	Project leadership and the schools of leadership	26
3-7	Success criteria and associated success factors after Wateridge (1995)	27
3-8	Project success criteria, interested stakeholders and timescales over which they make their judgment, after Turner (2004)	30
3-9	A simplified model for project categories	32
4-1	Fifteen leadership competencies, after Dulewicz and Higgs (2003)	33
4-2	Success criteria used for this study	33
4-3	Final model for project categorization used in the research	39
5-1	Countries from which the interviewees came	40
5-2	Industries from which the interviewees came	40
5-3	Success criteria and number of times mentioned	40
5-4	Criteria for selecting project managers and number of times mentioned	42
5-5	Rating of the leadership competencies of project managers	44
6-1	Results, all projects and the three types by application area	48
6-2	Results, complexity, all projects and three application areas, high-performing projects	50
6-3	Results, project importance, all projects and three application areas, high-performing projects	51
6-4	Results, contract type, all projects and three application areas, high-performing projects only	52
6-5a	Results, project phase, all projects and three application areas, high-performing only	54
6-5b	Results, project phase, IT projects and organizational projects, high-performing projects only	55
6-6	Results, culture, all projects and three application areas, high-performing projects only	56
6-7	Results and validation, all projects, high performance projects only	57
6-8	Results and validation, engineering projects, high-performance projects only	58
6-9	Results and validation, engineering projects, high-performance projects only	59
6-10	Results and validation, organizational change projects, high-performance projects only	60
6-11	Summary of important dimensions across three application areas	62

Appendices

C-1	Project categories after Crawford, Hobbs, and Turner (2005)	84
D-1	Categories of project types	86
D-2	Relative importance of importance of the project manager's characteristics	86
E-1	Organizations interviewed	89
E-2	Nature of projects in the organizations interviewed	90
E-3	Attributes of projects undertaken by the organizations interviewed	91
E-4	How the interviewees judged project success	94
E-5	Criteria mentioned by the interviewees for selecting project managers	95
E-6	Task versus people orientation of project managers	98
E-7	Rating of the leadership competencies of project managers	99
G-1	Sample demographics by job function	105
G-2	Sample demographics by nationality	106
G-3	Sample demographics by project management certification	106
G-4	Data descriptions of the fifteen competencies	107
G-5	Data descriptions of the calculated variables	108
G-6	Interviewee ratings of competencies, engineering projects	108
G-7	Interviewee ratings of competencies, IT projects	109
G-8	Interviewee ratings of competencies, organizational change projects	109
G-9	Significant differences in high-performing projects of different complexity	110
G-10	Significant differences in high-performing projects at different project life-cycle stages	111
G-11	Significant differences in high-performing projects using different contract types	111
G-12	Range, mean and standard deviation of sten codes from our sample	111

List of Figures

3-1	The Seven Forces Model for project success, after Turner (1999)	22
3-2	Project Excellence model, after Westerveld and Gaya-Walters (2001)	23
3-3	Reasons for categorizing projects, after Crawford, Hobbs, and Turner (2005)	28
3-4	Groups of attributes for categorizing projects, after Crawford, Hobbs, and Turner (2005)	29
4-1	Research model	32
7-1	Project manager profile on high-performing engineering projects	63
7-2	Project manager profile on high-performing IT projects	64
7-3	Project manager profile on high-performing organizational change projects	64
7-4	Project manager profile on high-performing, low-complexity projects	66
7-5	Project manager profile on high-performing, medium-complexity projects	66
7-6	Project manager profile on high-performing, high-complexity projects	67
7-7	Project manager profile on high-performing, mandatory projects	68
7-8	Project manager profile on high-performing, renewal projects	68
7-9	Project manager profile on high-performing, repositioning projects	69
7-10	Project manager profile on high-performing, alliance contract projects	70
7-11	Project manager profile on high-performing, remeasurement contract projects	70
7-12	Project manager profile on high-performing, fixed-price contract projects	71
7-13	Project manager profile on high-performing projects, covering design, execution, and close-out stage	72
7-14	Project manager profile on high-performing projects, covering design, execution, close-out, and commissioning stages	72
7-15	Project manager profile on high-performing projects, covering feasibility, design, execution, and close-out stages	73
7-16	Project manager profile on high-performing projects, covering feasibility, design, execution, close-out, and commissioning stages	73

Appendices

G-1	Response distribution over time	106

Executive Summary

There are two widely held beliefs in the project management community:
1. The first is that the project manager's competence makes no contribution to project success. As long as he or she uses the right tools and techniques the project will be successful. The project success literature almost studiously ignores the project manager.
2. The second is that as long as a given project manager has learned to apply those tools and techniques well, he or she can apply them to any type of project, regardless of technology, discipline, or domain.

Both these beliefs undervalue the project manager. They suggest that anybody, even the proverbial chimpanzee, can manage any project well, as long as they apply the right tools and techniques. The tools manage the project, not the person. This is in stark contrast to the general management literature where it has been shown over the last seventy years that the manager's competence makes a direct contribution to the success of the organization he or she manages, and different competency profiles are required in different circumstances. We should expect it to be the same in the temporary organization that is a project.

Competence can be defined as the knowledge, skills, and personal characteristics to achieve desired performance standards. Previous researchers have looked at the knowledge and skills required by project managers, but that has tended to reinforce the above beliefs. Knowledge is knowledge of the project management tools and techniques, and skill is the ability to apply them in any project context. However, a recent research project sponsored by PMI looked at project categorization, and concluded that two reasons why organization's categorize projects are to choose appropriate tools and techniques to manage their projects, and to choose the appropriate project manager for a given situation. Different subsets of the project management tools and techniques are required on different types of projects, and they need to be applied in different ways, and organizations recognize that different profiles of competence are required to manage different types of projects, and one project manager may be more competent than another.

In this research project we focus on the third dimension of competence, the personal characteristics, particularly leadership style. It is this third dimension that is identified by the general management literature as making the greatest contribution to a manager's leadership ability; it is personal characteristics, particularly emotional intelligence, that is the greatest differentiator. Accordingly, we set out to show that the project manager's competence, particularly their leadership style, does contribute to project success, and different competence profiles, particularly different leadership styles, are required on different types of project. We aim to answer the following two research questions:
1. Does the project manager's competence, including his or her leadership style, influence project success?
2. Are different competence profiles, including different leadership styles, appropriate for different types of project?

To answer these questions we conducted our research project in four stages:
1. We conducted a literature search.
2. We developed a research model.
3. We undertook semi-structured interviews with managers of project managers.
4. We conducted a Web-based questionnaire.

Literature search

We looked at two sets of literature, the general management literature on leadership, and the project management literature on project success. In the general management literature we looked at the six schools of leadership developed over the last seventy years, finishing with the competency school. From the competency school we adopted a model for leadership competence that uses fifteen dimensions of competency in three groups: emotional competence (EQ), managerial competence (MQ), and intellectual competence (IQ). The fifteen dimensions became the independent variables for our research model.

There are two elements of the project success literature, one looking at project success factors and the other at project success criteria. We reviewed the project success literature and discovered that it almost studiously ignores the project manager's contribution to project success. But it does not ignore his or her contribution completely, so we did review what has been written. From the project success literature we identified how people judge projects to be successful. Initially, we adopted a five-dimensional model, but we extended this to a ten-dimensional model as a result of our interviews. The ten dimensions became the dependent variables of our research model.

We also reviewed the results of PMI's recent research project into project categorization which provides a fourteen-attribute model to categorize projects, with limitless categories. This was too complex for our needs. We initially adopted a five-attribute model with sixteen categories of projects, but we extended that to a six-attribute model with nineteen categories as a result of our interviews and this became the moderating variable for our research model.

Research model

To answer our research questions we adopted two hypotheses.

Hypothesis 1:   The project manager's competency, which includes his or her leadership style, is positively correlated to project success.

Hypothesis 2:   Different combinations of project management competency are correlated with success on different types of projects.

To investigate these hypotheses we adopted a simple research model with:
- fifteen independent variables, the fifteen competency dimensions of leadership style
- ten independent variables, the ten dimensions of project success
- nineteen moderating variables, the nineteen categories of projects.

We tested Hypothesis 1 by seeing if certain profiles of the fifteen competency dimensions of leadership led to better project performance as judged by the ten dimensions of success. We tested Hypothesis 2 by seeing if different profiles led to better performance on different types of projects as judged by the nineteen categories of projects.

Interviews

We first conducted fourteen semi-structured interviews to test the model. The interviewees were managers of project managers, and came from eight countries and a range of industries. There were clients, contracting and consultancy companies, and people doing internal projects, and projects for external clients. We asked the interviewees:
- whether they could identify with the fifteen leadership competencies, and how they rated them in selecting project managers
- how they judged their projects to be successful
- how they categorized projects
- whether they considered the project manager's competency when selecting the manager for a project, and what was important to them.

Our interviewees did consider the project manager's leadership style when choosing the manager for a project, and often chose different types of managers for different types of projects. Particularly high complexity projects, whatever that meant for the organization, required appropriate leadership skills. Several organizations had a pool of project managers, and these decisions were made as people were appointed to the pool, not as they were appointed to individual projects. As a result of the interviews we made minor adjustments to the research model, as previously described.

Web-based questionnaire

Next, we conducted a Web-based questionnaire, to which we had 400 usable responses. We asked the respondents to categorize their last project against our nineteen project types, and to say how successful it was. We asked them to say how it performed against our ten success criteria, but also to say how important each criterion is. We then asked them to complete a psychometric test to judge their leadership style against the fifteen competency dimensions. We analyzed the responses in two ways:

1. We correlated the fifteen leadership competencies to performance on each type of project, and combinations of the project types, to determine which competency styles are important for project success for each type of project. We validated those results against the interviews.
2. We determined the profiles of the managers of high-performing projects against all fifteen competency dimensions for most of the nineteen types of projects (we were not able to obtain meaningful results for a small number of project types).

Conclusions

We found from the research that our hypotheses were supported, and thus we achieved an affirmative answer to our two research questions:

1. The project manager's competency, including his or her leadership style, is a contributor to project success.
2. Different competency profiles, including different leadership styles are appropriate for different types of projects.

We found the following leadership competencies had the greatest impact on success:
- conscientiousness and motivation for engineering projects
- communication and self-awareness for information systems projects
- communication and motivation for organizational change projects
- emotional resilience and communication for medium complexity projects
- sensitivity for high complexity projects
- developing for mandatory projects
- motivation for repositioning projects
- communication and self-awareness for renewal projects
- communication and sensitivity on fixed-price contracts
- communication and influence on remeasurement projects
- conscientiousness and communication throughout the project life cycle, with managing resources also important at design, and motivation and sensitivity at commissioning
- conscientiousness, sensitivity, managing resources and communication on multicultural projects.

A contentious finding is that vision in the project manager is negatively correlated with project success in many project types. Our interpretation of this is that the project manager must be focused on delivering the project as designed. It is the responsibility of other governance roles, such as the project sponsor, to make sure the project is linked to the strategy of the parent organization. It is the project manager's responsibility to focus on delivering the project, and not get distracted by the bright lights of vision.

Consistently with the general management literature we found that the emotional group of competencies, EQ, was the most significant for successful project outcomes. Project managers must be emotionally intelligent.

In looking at the profiles of the managers of successful programs, an interesting observation was the managers of IT and renewal projects had an almost identical profile, and the managers of repositioning and organizational change projects had very similar styles.

Our recommendation is that managers of project managers need to do three things:
1. Be aware of the appropriate leadership competencies when selecting project managers for projects.
2. Develop within the pool of project managers appropriate leadership competencies for the type of projects undertaken within the organization.
3. Appreciate their project managers and their contribution to the success of projects within the organization.

CHAPTER 1

Introduction

There are two strongly held beliefs pervading the project management community.

(a) The first is held by omission. There appears to be a belief that the project manager, and his or her competency and leadership style, make no contribution to project success. When we review the project success literature in Chapter 3, we show that it almost studiously ignores the project manager. It talks about the tools and techniques used, risk management, and communication with the client, project team and other stakeholders, but it does not mention the project manager. One might say that the project manager's competence is implied *en passant*. If it is said that good planning, good risk management, or good communication is a success factor; then by implication the project manager must be competent in those things and he or she must be competent for the project to be successful. But if the project manager is ignored, and as long as good, appropriate tools are used, the project will be successful regardless of the project manager's competence. As long as the right tools are used, the project can be managed by the proverbial chimpanzee. Perhaps this is one reason why project managers are so undervalued in some disciplines.

(b) The other is a tenet of project management, that once you have learned the skills of project management, you can manage any project, regardless of the technology and industry. This is the issue of domain knowledge, and people hold very strong opinions. Some say that to manage an information systems project you need to be an information systems professional, to manage the construction of a nuclear power station you need previous experience of the nuclear power industry. Others say, no, the tools of project management are generic, and once you have learned them they can be applied to any project. Most people within the project management community hold the latter view; the competent project manager can apply his or her skills to any project, regardless of technology. Interestingly, these discussions are almost always in terms of the technology. Can you apply your project management skills to managing an information systems project even if you know nothing about computers? Can you apply your project management skills to the construction of a nuclear power plant even if you know nothing about welding a nuclear reactor together? The discussions are never in terms of temperament. Do you have the temperament to manage a team of computer programmers? Do you have the temperament to stand on top of a nuclear reactor at two o'clock in the morning as the pressure test is being conducted?

These two beliefs may appear to be incompatible initially; the first is saying the project manager does not make any difference, while the second focuses on the project manager. But in fact they are two sides of the same coin. The first is saying that it is only the planning and control tools that make a difference, not the project manager and his or her competence and leadership style; while the second is saying that once someone knows how to apply the tools and techniques, they can apply them to any project, regardless of their domain knowledge and temperament, both of which are elements of their competence.

In a recent research project sponsored by PMI, Lynn Crawford, Brian Hobbs, and Rodney Turner have shown that one reason why organizations categorize projects is to be able to develop and choose appropriate project management methodologies for different types of projects (Crawford, Hobbs, and Turner 2005). But, if they use different project management methodologies for different types of projects, then surely they need to use project managers with different competency profiles on different types of projects! Thus, we conclude that unquestionably the success of the project must be dependent on the competence of the project manager, and that different profiles of skills and competence are appropriate for different types of projects.

Crawford (2001, 2003, 2005) defines competence as the knowledge, skills and personal characteristics required to achieve job performance as defined by appropriate standards. Thus, to manage the project effectively, the project manager needs knowledge about the application of project management tools and techniques, and not only the skill to apply them in routine situations, but also the competence to apply them in unfamiliar situations to be able to respond to unexpected situations. The project may also need technical knowledge of the project domain, and the skill to apply it.

The definition of competence also talks about personal characteristics. The project manager must have the appropriate temperament to manage this type of project. Perhaps, the reason an information systems professional is needed to manage an information systems project is that the project manager must understand what makes computer programmers tick; what motivates them; what aspirations they have; how they work. If one is managing the construction of a nuclear power station, one needs to know what it is like to be hung upside down on a nuclear reactor at two o'clock in the morning, trying to perform a precise technical weld, the failure of which can delay the program by months. If one is managing an environmental project as part of the Sydney Olympics in 2000, one needs to be able to communicate with Greenpeace and keep them onside, and communicate with highly intelligent but reticent academics to extract from them the science to make it work. (We shall see in Chapter 5 that the project required two project managers because both sets of communication skills could not be found in one person.) The project is dependent on the leadership style of the project manager, and different types of projects require different leadership styles and different temperaments.

In the general management arena, six schools of leadership have been developed over the last seventy years. All six schools suggest that a manager's leadership style influences the performance of his or her organization, and the last five suggest that different leadership styles are appropriate for different contexts. The general management literature says it is this third dimension of competence, the personal characteristics, and particularly leadership style, that is the main differentiator for performance as a manager. Against this background, it would be strange indeed if a project manager's leadership style did not influence the success of his or her project, and if it were not the case that different leadership styles are appropriate on different types of projects. Thus, we have undertaken this research project, sponsored by the Project Management Institute, to answer the following two questions:

1. Does the project manager's competence, including his or her leadership style, influence project success?
2. Are different competence profiles, including different leadership styles, appropriate for different types of projects?

The research project

In order to answer these two questions we conducted two surveys. First, we developed a research model. We wished to test whether certain leadership styles are more likely to lead to the successful outcome of projects, and whether different profiles of leadership styles are more successful on different types of projects. From the general management literature we identified a fifteen-dimensional model for leadership competence, with fifteen competencies grouped into three competence groups: Emotional Quotient (EQ), Managerial Quotient (MQ), and Intellectual Quotient (IQ). We also needed to define what we meant by project success. We started with five qualitative criteria of project success, but expanded that to ten based on our interviews. We were then ready to answer the first question. To answer the second we needed to identify different project types. From the work of Crawford, Hobbs, and Turner (2005), we identified nineteen types of projects, grouped into six attribute areas. Using those we determined whether, for those nineteen different types of projects, different profiles of the fifteen leadership competencies were appropriate for the nineteen types of projects. However, we were also able to combine the nineteen different types to obtain a much wider range of types of projects.

We were then ready to conduct our two surveys.
1. The first was a series of interviews with managers responsible for appointing project managers to projects. We asked them whether they could identify with our research model, the leadership dimensions, the measures of success, and the types of projects. We asked the interviewees to rate the fifteen leadership dimensions to compare with the results from our questionnaire later. All could identify with the leadership dimensions. But based on the interviews we expanded the measures of success from five to ten, and the number of types of projects from sixteen to nineteen. Based on the interviews we added three contract types. We also asked the interviewees whether they considered the project manager's competence and leadership style when appointing them. They all said they did. Sometimes

they considered project management competence, sometimes domain competence, and sometimes leadership style. Several said they made the decisions when appointing people to the pool of project managers, but once someone is in the pool, they can manage any project the organization undertakes.
2. The second survey was a Web-based questionnaire. This was aimed at project management professionals. We asked the respondents to answer two sets of questions. The first set asked them to describe the last project they worked on, to rate its success, and to categorize it against the nineteen types. The second set of questions determined their profile against the fifteen leadership competencies. We were then able to determine if different profiles of leadership styles were more appropriate on different types of projects. We found across the board that project managers rate high on the emotional quotient (EQ). Somewhat to our surprise we found they rate low on the intellectual quotient (IQ), but this was consistent with the results from the interviews. Looking at the individual competencies we found the following had the greatest impact on success:
   - conscientiousness and motivation for engineering projects
   - communication and self-awareness for information systems projects
   - communication and motivation for organizational change projects
   - emotional resilience and communication for medium complexity projects
   - sensitivity for high complexity projects
   - developing for mandatory projects
   - motivation for repositioning projects
   - communication and self-awareness for renewal projects
   - communication and sensitivity on fixed-price contracts
   - communication and influence on remeasurement projects
   - conscientiousness and communication throughout the project life cycle, with managing resources also important at the design stage, and motivation and sensitivity at commissioning
   - conscientiousness, sensitivity, managing resources and communication on multicultural projects.

Based on the results from the web-based questionnaire, we were also able to determine more detailed profiles of all fifteen leadership dimensions for the managers of high performing projects of most types of projects.

Thus, we concluded that the two hypotheses were supported, that the project manager's leadership style does influence success, and that different leadership styles are appropriate on different types of projects. The messages for the managers of projects are as follows:
1. When appointing project managers to projects, they should consider their leadership style and appoint project managers with appropriate leadership styles for the projects they have to manage.
2. They understand the types of projects the organization is undertaking, develop within the pool of available project managers' appropriate leadership styles for those projects. This may require the psychometric testing of project managers, and the implementation of training and development programs to develop the appropriate styles. It may also require psychometric testing of project managers as they are appointed to the pool.
3. They should value their project managers. The project manager's competence does contribute to project success, and so competent project managers should be valued.

The research was undertaken from December 2004 to March 2006. It was initiated and sponsored by the Project Management Institute. It was also supported by the Lille School of Management and by the Umeå School of Business, Umeå University.

Structure of this report

This report describes the results of our research project, and is structured as follows:

Chapter 2: Describes what the general management literature says about leadership. It describes the six schools of leadership, and how they are reflected in the project management literature. It discusses personality and how one is born with personality, but can adapt it to obtain an appropriate leadership style in different situations. Personality also relates to a person's performance as a project team member and we discuss why that is not the same thing as a leadership style. We expand further on how some of the schools say that different leadership styles are appropriate in different circumstances. We use one school, the competence school, to provide our fifteen leadership competencies.

Chapter 3: Reviews the project success literature. We describe what we mean by success factors, and how the project manager is usually not recognized as one of them. We also describe how project success is judged in choosing the model for our research. We review in detail what the project management literature says about the project manager's leadership style on different types of projects, and their contribution to success. We then describe how to categorize projects to provide the third element of our research model.

Chapter 4: Describes our methodology. We convert our two research questions into two hypotheses, and then describe our research model in more detail. We explain how we conducted the interviews, how we conducted the web-based questionnaire, and how we analyzed and validated the results.

Chapter 5: Describes results of the interviews. We describe the views of the interviewees on the three components of our research model and how they rated the fifteen competencies.

Chapter 6: Presents the results of the web-based questionnaire. We analyze the data for different types of projects to determine significant correlations between project performance and the three competence groups, EQ, MQ, and IQ, and the fifteen competency dimensions. We present the results for individual project types and combinations of them.

Chapter 7: Presents the project manager profiles in high performing projects against the fifteen competency dimensions.

Chapter 8: Presents our final conclusions and recommendations. We also suggest possible future research, and ask whether the research needs to be repeated for other project roles such as the project sponsor.

Appendix A: Gives the authors' contact details.

Appendix B: Describes the definition of the fifteen leadership competencies used as independent variables in the study.

Appendix C: Gives a full list of the fourteen project attributes suggested by Crawford, Hobbs, and Turner (2005) for categorizing projects, and some categories within each attribute. The six attributes and nineteen categories used as moderating variables were drawn from this list.

Appendix D: Presents the questions used in the semi-structured interviews.

Appendix E: Shows data from the interviews.

Appendix F: Presents the Web-based questionnaire.

Appendix G: Contains data from the Web-based questionnaire, and describes how it was analyzed, both to correlate the fifteen competency dimensions to project success, and to determine the profiles of managers of high performing projects.

In considering whether the project manager's leadership style influence project success, and whether different styles are appropriate on different projects, it is natural to start by considering first what has been written over the years about what constitutes good leadership, and whether different leadership styles have ever been found to be better in different contexts.

CHAPTER 2

Leadership

The aim of this research is to determine whether the project manager's leadership style or personality has an impact on project success, and whether that is different in different project situations. We start by investigating what the general management literature has said about what constitutes good leadership, and how that is reflected in the project management literature. We then consider what has been said about the appropriateness of different leadership styles in different contexts. In this chapter we also differentiate between what has been written about leadership and behaviors in teams, and consider the difference between leadership and personality.

The schools of leadership

Table 2-1 shows the six main schools of leadership that have developed over the past seventy years. It also shows three historical schools that demonstrate that the recent schools are founded in a great historical tradition.

Historical schools

Throughout history people have attempted to say what makes a good leader. Some of the most often quoted historical authors include Plato, Machiavelli, Hobbes, and Locke from the West (see, for instance, Collinson 1998), and Confucius and Xunxi from the East (see, for instance, Collinson, Plan, and Wilkinson 2000). As early as 500 B.C. Confucius listed the virtues (*de*) of effective leaders. Four were central to his beliefs:
- *jen* (love, or concern for relationships)
- *li* (proper conduct, or concern for process)
- *xiao* (piety, or values)
- *zhang rong* (the doctrine of the mean, or a concern for moderation).

The first three of these have remained central to leadership thinking for the subsequent 2,500 years. What has been lost is the doctrine of the mean, the Goldilocks principle. Everything should be done in moderation, and not too fanatically one way or the other. Aristotle also showed a similar approach with his three tenets:
- *pathos* (empathy, or concern for relationships)
- *ethos* (values)
- *logos* (logic, or concern for process).

This idea has been discussed by Stephen Covey (1992), who suggests that in the West *managers* tend to leap straight in with the logic, "You must do this because . . . !" He suggests that as a *leader*, first you need to build relationships with your team, then sell your values, and then and only then can you persuade them to follow you.

Schools of leadership in the 20th century

Barnard (1938) wrote a very early work on the role of the chief executive as both manager and leader. He suggested that an executive had both managerial and emotional functions, which he called cognitive and cathectic, respectively:
- cognitive functions include guiding, directing, and constraining choices and actions, (mainly a concern for process)
- cathectic functions include emotional and motivational aspects of goal setting, and developing faith and commitment in a larger moral purpose (mainly a concern for relationships).

School	Period	Main idea	Example authors
Confucius	500 B.C.	Relationships (*jen*) Values (*xiao*) Process (*li*) Moderation (*zhang rong*)	Chen (1990)
Aristotle	300 B.C.	Relationships (*pathos*) Values (*ethos*) Process (*logos*)	Collinson (1998); Covey (1992)
Barnard	1938	Relationships versus process	Barnard (1938)
Trait	1930s–1940s	Effective leaders show common traits Leaders born not made	Kirkpatrick and Locke (1992)
Behavior or style	1940s–1950s	Effective leaders adopt certain styles or behaviors Leadership skills can be developed	Adair (1983); Blake and Mouton (1978); Tannenbaum and Schmidt (1958)
Contingency	1960s–1970s	What makes an effective leader depends on the situation	Fiedler (1967); House (1971); Robbins (1997)
Visionary or charismatic	1980s–1990s	Two styles: Transformational: concern for relationships Transactional: concern for process	Bass (1990)
Emotional intelligence	2000s	Emotional intelligence has a greater impact on performance than intellect	Goleman, Boyatzis, and McKee (2002)
Competency	2000s	Effective leaders exhibit certain competencies, including traits, behaviors, and styles Three groups of competencies: emotions, intellect, and process Different profiles of competency better in different situations	Dulewicz and Higgs (2003)

Table 2-1   The schools of leadership

Throughout the twentieth century there were four main schools of leadership theory (Handy 1982; Partington 2003):
1. the trait school
2. the behavioral or style school
3. the contingency school
4. the visionary or charismatic school.

As we move into the twenty-first century, two additional schools have developed building on those four schools:
5. the emotional intelligence school (Goleman, Boyatzis, and McKee 2002)
6. the competence school (see, for instance, Dulewicz and Higgs 2003).

The trait school

The trait school was popular up to the 1940s. The idea is that effective leaders share common traits. It effectively assumes that leaders are born not made. Attempts to identify the traits of effective leaders have focused on three main areas:
- abilities: hard management skills
- personality: such self-confidence and emotional variables
- physical appearance: including size and appearance.

Kirkpatrick and Locke (1991) also identified six traits of effective leaders:
- drive and ambition
- desire to lead and influence others
- honesty and integrity
- self-confidence

- intelligence
- technical knowledge.

The project management literature has tried to identify the traits of effective project managers. Through his work at Henley Management College, Rodney Turner (1999) identified seven:
- problem-solving ability
- results orientation
- energy and initiative
- self-confidence
- perspective
- communication
- negotiating ability.

The behavioral or style school

The behavioral or style school was popular from the 1940s to the 1960s. It assumed that effective leaders adopt certain styles or behaviors. It assumes in effect that leadership skills can be developed (see, for instance, Blake and Mouton 1978; Tannenbaum and Schmidt 1958; Adair 1983; Hershey and Blanchard 1988; Slevin 1989). Most of the best-known theories characterize leaders against one or two parameters, and place them on a one-dimensional continuum or in a two-dimensional matrix; see Table 2-2. The parameters include:
1. Concern for people or relationships
2. Concern for production
3. Use of authority
4. Involvement of the team in decision-making (formulating decisions)
5. Involvement of the team in decision-taking (choosing options)
6. Flexibility versus the application of rules.

Adair (1983) produced the simplest model, saying that the leader should show concern for the task, the team and individuals in the team, covering parameters 2, 4, and 5, and 1, respectively. Blake and Mouton (1978) developed a two-dimensional grid based on concern for people and concern for production. They graded each parameter on a scale of 1 to 9 and identified five management styles, which also recognize the use of authority:
- impoverished (1,1)
- authority obedience (1,9)
- country club (9,1)
- compromise (5,5)
- team leader (9,9).

In reality they are management styles and not leadership styles. Bonoma and Slevin (Slevin, 1989) developed a two-dimensional grid based on how much the team is involved in decision-making and how little the team is involved in decision-taking. They graded each parameter on a scale of 0 to 100 and identified four management styles, which also encompass the use of authority:
- shareholder (0,0)
- consensus manager (100,0)
- autocrat (100,0)
- consultative autocrat (100,100).

The project management literature has identified styles of project leaders. Turner (1999), following Frame (1987), identified four styles based on parameters 4 to 6; see Table 2-3.

Parameter	Blake and Mouton	Tannenbaum and Schmidt	Hershey and Blanchard	Bonoma and Slevin
1. People 2. Production 3. Authority 4. Decision-making 5. Decision-taking	2-D grid based on 1 & 2 covering 3	1-D spectrum based on 3 covering 4 & 5	2-D grid based on 1 & 2 covering 3	2-D grid based on 4 & 5 covering 3

Table 2-2 Models of leadership style based on five parameters

Parameter	Laissez-faire	Democratic	Autocratic	Bureaucratic
4. Team decision-making	High	High	Low	Low
5. Team decision-taking	High	Low	Low	Low
6. Flexibility	High	High	High	Low

Table 2-3   Four styles of project leader (Turner 1999)

The contingency school

Most of the behavioral models suggest that different styles are appropriate in different circumstances. The contingency school, which was popular during the 1960s and 1970s, formalized that. Rather than seeking universal theories of leadership that would apply in every situation, contingency theories suggested that what made an effective leader would depend on the situation. This arose because it became clear that neither trait theories nor style theories described what made an effective leader in all circumstances. Most of the contingency theories tend to follow the same pattern:
1. Assess the characteristics of the leader
2. Evaluate the situation in terms of key contingency variables
3. Seek a match between the leader and the situation

One contingency theory that has proved popular is path-goal theory (House, 1971). The idea is that the leader must help the team find the path to their goals and help them in that process. Path-goal theory identifies four leadership behaviors:
- directive leaders
- supportive leaders
- participative leaders
- achievement-oriented leaders.

These must then be matched to environmental and subordinate contingency factors:
- environmental factors: task structure, formal authority system, work group
- subordinate factors: locus of control, experience, perceived ability

Robbins (1997) suggests how the different leadership styles may be selected in different circumstances, based on empirical evidence:
1. The directive style is appropriate when:
   - there is ambiguity
   - there is conflict in the work group
   - subordinates have little control over their destiny (external locus of control) and will be inappropriate when:
     - subordinates are very capable
     - there are clear, bureaucratic and formal authority relationships.
2. The supportive style is appropriate when:
   - subordinates are performing structured tasks
   - there are clear, bureaucratic and formal authority relationships.
3. The participative style is appropriate when:
   - subordinates can control their destiny (internal locus of control).
4. The achievement-oriented style is appropriate when:
   - subordinates are set challenging goals.

In the project management field, Frame (1987) suggested how the four leadership styles listed in Table 2-3 are appropriate at different stages of the project life-cycle and with different team structures, also see Table 2.4.

The visionary or charismatic school

The visionary school was popular during the 1980s and 1990s and arose from the study of successful business leaders leading their organizations through change. Bass (1990) identified two types of leadership, transactional and transformational:
1. Transactional leadership (concern for process)
   - emphasizes contingent rewards, rewarding followers for meeting performance targets
   - manages by exception, taking action when tasks are not proceeding according to plan.

Leadership style	Stage	Team type	Team nature
Laissez-faire	Feasibility	Egoless	Experts with shared responsibility
Democratic	Design	Matrix	Mixed discipline working on several tasks
Autocratic	Execution	Task	Single discipline working on separate tasks
Bureaucratic	Close-out	Surgical	Mixed working on a single task

Table 2-4   Leadership styles, project team types, and the project life cycle

2. Transformational leadership (concern for relationships)
   - exhibits charisma, developing a vision, engendering pride, respect and trust
   - provides inspiration, motivating by creating high expectations and modeling appropriate behaviors
   - gives consideration to the individual, paying personal attention to followers and giving them respect and personality
   - provides intellectual stimulation, challenging followers with new ideas and approaches.

The transactional leader emphasizes Barnard's cognitive roles and Aristotle's *logos*. The transformational leader emphasizes Barnard's cathectic roles, Aristotle's *pathos* and *ethos*. In reality a different combination of the two styles will be appropriate in different circumstances. There are four stages of visionary leadership:
1. Identify the opportunity and need for change and formulate a vision
2. Communicate the vision and the unacceptable nature of the status quo
3. Build trust in the vision
4. Lead by example

In a project management context, Keegan and Den Hartog (2004) predicted that transformational leadership would be more appropriate for project managers. However, in their study, although they found a preference for transformational leadership, they could find no significant link. Thus, across all projects, that one dimension was not a significant determinant of success as a project manager. However, based on our results reported later, we would predict that they would find a transformational leadership style preferred on complex change projects and a transactional style preferred on simple, engineering projects.

The emotional intelligence school

The emotional intelligence school has been popular since the late 1990s, and says the leader's emotional intelligence has a greater impact on his or her success as a leader and the performance of his or her team than his or her intellectual capability (Goleman, Boyatzis, and McKee 2002). Goleman et al. identified four dimensions of emotional intelligence (see Table 2-5), and from there six leadership styles:
- visionary
- coaching
- affiliative
- democratic
- pacesetting
- commanding.

They say the first four foster resonance in the team, and usually lead to better performance in appropriate circumstances. The last two they describe as toxic, and say can foster dissonance, so should only be used in turnaround situations. Through a study of 4,000 chief executives, Goleman et al. have shown a clear correlation between the emotional intelligence and leadership style of managers and the performance of their organizations.

Lee-Kelley, Leong, and Loong (2003) set out to find which project management knowledge areas are critical to project success and whether the project manager's leadership style influences his or her perception of control. What they found was the project manager's leadership style influenced his or her perception of success on the project. They suggest the following:

> "[There is] a significant relationship between the leader's perception of project success and his or her personality and contingent experiences. Thus the inner confidence and self-belief from personal knowledge and experience are likely to play an important role in a manager's ability to deliver a project successfully" (p. 590).

Domains	Competencies
Personal Competence	
• self-awareness	emotional self-awareness accurate self-assessment self-confidence
• self-management	emotional self-control transparency adaptability achievement initiative optimism
Social Competence	
• social awareness	empathy organizational awareness service
• relationship management	inspirational leadership influence developing others change catalyst conflict management building bonds teamwork and collaboration

Table 2-5   Domains of emotional intelligence

It seems that the project manager's emotional intelligence has an impact on his or her perception of the success of the project. Emotional intelligence comprises four components as shown in Table 2-5. All four of those could impinge on a project manager's perception of success of his or her project:
(a) How aware is he or she of his or her performance on the project, not whether he or she thought the project was a success (it achieved its key performance indicators), but whether he or she thought the project management was a success—is he or she satisfied with how he or she managed the project
(b) That assessment may be influenced by how the manager felt he or she comported himself or herself
(c) The satisfaction of the project team members may also affect the manager's assessment of the project, regardless of how the project actually performed
(d) The satisfaction of the other stakeholders, particularly the client, may also have an effect.

The competency school of leadership

The focus of leadership research is now into the competence of leaders, and competencies they exhibit (see, for instance, Bass and Avolio 1995; Bennis 1989; Kotter 1990; Marshall 1991; Kouznes and Posner 1998; Goffee and Jones 2000; Alimo-Metcalfe and Alban-Metcalfe 2001; Zaccaro, Rittman, and Marks 2001; Goleman, Boyatzis, and McKee 2002; Kets de Vries and Florent-Treacy 2002; Dulewicz and Higgs 2003). Because it forms the basis of our research model, we devote a separate section to it.

Competence and the earlier schools

At first sight it might appear that the competence school signals a return to the trait school. However, in reality, the competence school encompasses all of the earlier schools. Competence can be defined as the following (Boyatsis 1982; Crawford 2003):
- knowledge
- skills
- personal characteristics

required to achieve job performance as defined by appropriate standards.

Competence includes personal characteristics (traits as understood by the traits school and emotional intelligence), and knowledge and skills (including intelligence and problem-solving ability as well as management skill). The competence school therefore covers traits and styles. But it goes on to show that different competence profiles are appropriate in different circumstances, covering the contingency school. Finally, personal characteristics also encompass charisma and vision, and it is possible to build different competency profiles to match different forms of leadership such as transactional and transformational leadership.

Types of competence

Dulewicz and Higgs (2003) show many of the authors identify up to four types of competencies that determine leadership performance (see, for instance, Marshall 1991; Zaccaro, Rittman, and Marks 2001; Kets de Vries and Florent-Treacy 2002):
1. Cognitive
2. Emotional
3. Behavioral
4. Motivational.

Cognitive competencies are related to Barnard's cognitive functions of the executive, and Confucius's *li*. Emotional, behavioral and motivational are related to Barnard's cathectic functions, and Confucius's *ren* and *yi*. (How far have we come in 2,500 years?) However, based on their own observations and their analysis of the literature Dulewicz and Higgs (2003) suggest that three types of competence explain most of managerial performance:
- intellectual (IQ)
- managerial (MQ)
- emotional (EQ).

From this list they have broken cognitive into intellectual (intelligence and problem-solving abilities) and managerial (knowledge and skills of management functions). Emotional, behavioral, and motivational (Barnard's cathectic functions) have been combined into one. Elsewhere, Dulewicz and Higgs (2000) show that intellectual competence (IQ) accounts for 27% of leadership performance, managerial competence (MQ) accounts for 16%, and emotional competence (EQ) accounts for 36%. Emotional competence is therefore the most significant, but the other two are important as Barnard and Confucius suggested.

Leadership competencies

From their review of the literature (Bass and Avolio 1995; Bennis 1989; Kotter 1990; Kouznes and Posner 1998; Goffee and Jones, 2000; Alimo-Metcalfe and Alban-Metcalfe 2001; Goleman, Boyatzis, and McKee 2002) Dulewicz and Higgs (2003) have identified fifteen leadership competencies. There are seven emotional (EQ) competencies, three intellectual (IQ), and five managerial (MQ); see Table 2-6. By tabulating their fifteen competencies against those suggested by the other authors, they show there is quite strong agreement in the literature to this list. Other authors have slightly fewer or slightly more competencies on their list. They

Group	Competency	Goal	Involving	Engaging
Intellectual (IQ)	1. critical analysis and judgment 2. vision and imagination 3. strategic perspective	High High High	Medium High Medium	Medium Medium Medium
Managerial (MQ)	4. engaging communication 5. managing resources 6. empowering 7. developing 8. achieving	Medium High Low Medium High	Medium Medium Medium Medium Medium	High Low High High Medium
Emotional (EQ)	9. self-awareness 10. emotional resilience 11. motivation 12. sensitivity 13. influence 14. intuitiveness 15. conscientiousness	Medium High High Medium Medium Medium High	High High High Medium High Medium High	High High High High High High High

Table 2-6 Fifteen leadership competencies as suggested by Dulewicz and Higgs (2003), and the competency profiles of three leadership styles

merge some and split some, however, there is strong agreement to the list. Dulewicz and Higgs's definitions of their fifteen competencies are given in Appendix B.

Styles (and charisma)
Dulewicz and Higgs (2003) identify three leadership styles:
1. Engaging (E)
2. Involving (I)
3. Goal-oriented (G)

These styles are similar to the four styles of path-goal theory (House 1971) and the two styles from the visionary school (Bass 1990). So although these are offered as styles, they are related to the styles of the competence and visionary schools more than those of the style schools. These styles show different competence profiles as shown in Table 2-6.

Contingency
Dulewicz and Higgs (2003) go on to show that leaders with the different leadership styles perform better or worse on different types of change projects; (see Table 2-7). Thus, their fifteen leadership dimensions can be used to explain the performance of project managers on different types of change projects, and it is therefore suggested that they are adopted for the present study. However, different ways of categorizing project manager styles, with different profiles of competency, may be appropriate for different project attributes. In the next section we review what the general management literature has said about matching type of leader to different management scenarios.

The project management literature on competence
In the project management context, Crawford (2001, 2005) investigated the competence of project managers, and found different competence profiles appropriate for different types of projects. However, she did not investigate leadership style per se. In the construction management context, Dainty, Cjeng, and Moore (2005) identified twelve behavioral competencies associated with the construction project management role. They reduce these to two core competencies, team leadership and self-control.

Cultural behaviors of leaders
Before moving on to consider in more detail what the general manager has to say about leadership performance in different contexts, we look briefly at another dimension used to explain the performance of leaders: their cultural preferences. This tends to be presented as an environmental factor, with different styles being appropriate in different cultural contexts. The most commonly quoted cultural preferences are due to Hofstede (1991) and Trompenaars (1993); see Table 2-8. Although these are environmental factors, many are related to the parameters determining styles of managers in the style school and in path-goal theory.

In a project management context, many authors have written about the leadership styles appropriate on multicultural projects (for instance, see Björkman and Schaap 1992; Hastings and Briner 1996; Turner 1999; Selmer 2002; Rees 2003; Mäkilouko 2004; Mäller and Turner 2004). Selmer (2002) suggests personality traits for coping with cultural differences:
- agreeableness
- conscientiousness
- emotional stability
- intellect
- openness/extroversion.

Leadership style	Relatively Stable	Context Significant Change	Transformational Change
Goal-oriented	Good fit	Moderate fit	Poor fit
Involving	Moderate fit	Good fit	Moderate fit
Engaging	Poor fit	Moderate fit	Good fit

Table 2-7   Performance of different leadership styles on different types of change projects

Author	Cultural dimension	Explanation
Hofstede	Power distance Individualism vs. collectivism Uncertainty avoidance Masculinity	Autocracy vs. democracy, range of influence Focus on individual or group Attitude to risk, complexity and ambiguity Differentiation of male and female roles
Trompenaars	Universalist vs. particularist Specific vs. diffuse Neutral vs. emotional Short term vs. long term Achievement vs. ascription Attitudes to time Internal vs. external	Ethics and personal relationships Legal processes and trust Objective vs. emotional Perspective of investment returns and results Status, performance, assignment of rewards Emphasis on past, present, and future Ego versus society

Table 2-8   Cultural dimensions of leadership after Hofstede (1991) and Trompenaars (1993)

Mäkilouko (2004) suggests most project managers adopt task-oriented styles, which are inappropriate in multicultural situations, but suggest some project managers adopt two other more appropriate styles, people-oriented and relationship-oriented. Müller and Turner (2004) have shown a correlation between the cultural preferences of project managers and their performance in different contexts.

Leadership styles and context

This research project is about trying to identify whether different project leadership styles are appropriate on different types of projects, so it is worthwhile to consider in more detail what the general management literatures says about whether different leadership styles are appropriate in different general management contexts. We previously described the theories of leadership from the last 70 years, identifying six main schools. Most of the work on leadership under different contexts has been done under the contingency or visionary schools.

Functional or group approach

The leadership approach developed by Krech, Crutchfield, and Ballachey (1962) as part of the contingency school shows the complexity of leadership in different contexts by categorizing the roles and responsibilities leaders are expected to fulfill. Their approach assumes a team to execute the leadership functions by having the best suitable person on the team executing a leadership task. They identify fourteen functions; see Table 2-9. This approach focuses not on the individual, but on the leadership function per se. The context for leadership is set by each task. The team leader as well as the members of the team will exert leadership alike if that is needed. This approach does not change the existing paradigms for leadership and its dimensions, but adds a fit-for-task dimension based on interchangeable resources. The improved fit of individual to task is then balanced by the increased need for coordination and communication among the team members. Although this theory says it is about leadership functions it focuses more on roles fulfilled by team members. But everybody on a team can fulfill a leadership role.

Fiedler's contingency model

Fiedler (1967) recommends different leadership styles, depending on the favorability of the leadership situation. He identified three major variables to determine this favorability, which then affects the leader's role and influence. These are as follows:
- **Leader-member relations**: degree the leader is trusted and liked by the members.
- **Task structure**: degree of clearness of a task and its instructions.
- **Position power**: leader power by virtue of organizational position.

Fiedler distinguishes between task-oriented and participative approaches to leadership. He uses a least-preferred-coworker (LPC) score to assign team members to leaders depending on the leadership situation. In very favorable situations (good leader-member relations, structured task, strong position power) and very unfavorable situations (poor leader-member relations, unstructured tasks, weak position), he assigns **task-oriented leaders** (having a low LPC score) to achieve effectiveness through a directive and controlling style. In moderately favorable situations (all variables mixed) he assigns **participative leaders** (high LPC score) for high effectiveness through interpersonal relationship orientation.

Leadership role	Leadership responsibility
Executive	Top-coordinator, overseeing policy execution
Planner	For both short-term and long-term plans
Policy-maker	Establishing group goals and policies
Expert	Source of information and skills
External group representative	Official spokesperson
Controller of internal relations	Determining aspects of group structure
Purveyor of rewards and punishment	Controlling the group through power
Arbitrator and mediator	Controlling interpersonal conflict
Exemplar	Role model for group behavior
Symbol of the group	Providing focus for the group as distinct entity
Substitute for individual responsibility	Relieves individuals from personal responsibility
Ideologist	A source of beliefs, values, and standards
Father figure	Object of identification and transference
Scapegoat	Target for aggression, hostility, and blame

Table 2-9   Fourteen leadership functions according to Krech, Crutchfield, and Ballachey (1962)

Leadership styles at different stages of the business

The need for different leadership styles at different stages in the development of a business organization was identified by Clarke and Pratt (1985). They identified four different styles along the organizational migration:
- **Champion**: fighting for and defending the seedling business. Requires a broad set of leadership skills.
- **Tank commander**: team developer to sustain the growth period. Requires a team builder as leader.
- **Housekeeper**: efficient and economic resource usage in mature stage of the business. Requires planning and controlling skills in the leader.
- **Lemon-squeezer**: extracting the maximum from a declining business. Requires a tough and innovative leader to cut costs and improve productivity.

Clarke and Pratt suggested that most managers are only one or two of the four required types of leaders, thus, the need for different leaders at different stages of the business.

Along the same lines, Rodrigues (1988) identified three stages of development for organizations in dynamic environments. The stages are as follows:
- problem-solving stage
- implementation of solution stage
- stable stage.

With respect to the three stages, three different leadership styles are needed for effective leadership at each stage:
- **Innovator**: searching for new ideas and ways to control and manipulate the environment.
- **Implementer**: controlling and influencing the situation, accomplishing things through people.
- **Pacifier**: building friendly atmosphere and social interaction to pacify important individuals, using a less directive style than innovator or implementer.

Slevin (1989) developed a similar model showing different styles of management and organizational context, appropriate at different stages of product development, that can be related to the Boston Consulting Product Portfolio Matrix (Turner 1999); see Table 2-10.

These theories underline the need to change leadership styles contingent on the context at any given time. They support the view of the visionary school that both transactional and transformational leadership styles are necessary for effective leadership (Bass 1990).

Context dependency and the multifactor leadership questionnaire (MLQ)

Derived from the charismatic school, the MLQ (Bass 1990) is the widest used leadership assessment questionnaire that tests transactional, transformational, and non-transactional laissez-faire leadership style. The underlying dimensions are shown in Table 2-11. Antonakis, Avolio, and Sivasubramaniam (2003) identified

Slevin (1989) Management Style		Boston Consulting Matrix Competitive Advantage			
		High	Low		
	Entrepreneurial	*Rising stars* Consolidation **Commander**	*Problem children* Entrepreneurial **Champion**	High	Boston Consulting Matrix Market Growth
	Conservative	*Cash cows* Bureaucratic **Housekeeper**	*Dogs* Dissolution **Lemon squeezer**	Low	
		Mechanistic	Organic		
		Organizational Structure Slevin (1989)			

Notes:
Italics: Stage of product development according to the Boston Consulting Product Portfolio Matrix
Normal: Management style according to Slevin (1989)
Bold: Management style according to Clark and Pratt (1985)

Table 2-10   Management style versus product portfolio and life cycle

Style	Dimensions	Description
Transformational	Idealized influence (attributed)	Charisma of the leader
	Idealized influence (behavior) Inspirational motivation Intellectual stimulation Individualized consideration	Charisma centered on values, beliefs, and mission Energizing followers by optimism, goals, and vision Challenging creativity for problem-solving Advising, supporting, and caring for individuals
Transactional	Contingent reward leadership Management by exception (active) Management by exception (passive)	Providing role, task clarification, and psychological rewards Active vigilance of a leader to ensure goals are met Leader's intervention after mistakes happened
Laissez-faire	Laissez-faire leadership	Leader avoids making decisions, abdicates responsibility, and does not use authority

Table 2-11   Dimensions of the multifactor leadership questionnaire (Bass 1990)

the impact of context on the MLQ results. Contextual factors identified were environmental risk, leader's hierarchical level, and gender. Studies showed that reliable results can be achieved if the questionnaire is constrained to, and the results interpreted within, one of five business contexts:
- high risk
- stable business
- majority males
- majority females
- low-level leaders.

Dulewicz and Higgs (2004) showed the need to integrate contextual concepts in the MLQ and added scales for organizational commitment and organizational context. These contain four items designed to assess the degree of commitment that followers show to the organization and to the team in which they work, and one item to measure the extent of change faced by the organization. These items cover the following:
- job satisfaction
- realism
- commitment to requisite change and to the organization
- understanding the need for change
- change faced by the organization.

Their questionnaire removes the weaknesses identified within the original version of MLQ and provide for the broadest coverage in assessing leadership and context simultaneously.

Personality and team behaviors

In addition to the literature on the styles and behaviors of leaders, there is a substantial amount of literature on the behavior of team members. Sometimes people apply team roles to leadership styles. However, Dulewicz and Higgs (2003) have shown that there is little correlation between competencies of leaders and commonly identified team roles and behaviors. However, many of these are used as the basis for psychometric testing to determine the personality and behaviors of team members and team leaders to judge how they will perform, and as part of the recruitment of managers and executives. We describe five of the most commonly discussed theories.

FIRO-B

FIRO-B stands for Fundamental Interpersonal Relations Orientation-Behavior, and was developed by Schultz (1955). It examines the way people react with each other, looking at three types of work behaviors:
- *Inclusion*: social skills and the need to get on with other people.
- *Control*: leadership behavior, and how much control someone wants to exert and how much they are willing to receive.
- *Affection*: the deep need for giving and receiving affection.

FIRO-B also offers two other scores: the interpersonal score and expression of anger score. Used by the best practitioners FIRO-B can give an accurate picture of how an individual behaves at work and how he or she is perceived by others.

16PF

Cattell, Eber, and Tatsuoka (1970) identified sixteen personality factors (16PF) that influence a person's performance in a team; see Table 2-12. They grouped the sixteen factors into three groups:
1. Those showing extroversion versus introversion
2. Those showing emotional stability
3. Others.

Belbin

Belbin (1986) identified nine team roles, and associated characteristics; see Table 2-13. Dulewicz (1995) has correlated the Belbin team roles and 16PF showing that people adopting certain team roles exhibit particular personality factors.

Group	Factors
Extroversion	1. Outgoing 2. Assertive 3. Happy-go-lucky 4. Venturesome 5. Self-sufficient
Emotional stability	6. Anxious 7. Suspicious 8. Apprehensive 9. Controlled 10. Tense
Others	11. Intelligent 12. Conscientious 13. Tender minded 14. Imaginative 15. Shrewd 16. Experimenting

Table 2-12   The sixteen personality factors after Cattell, Eber, and Tatsuoka (1970)

Team Role	Characteristics	Team contribution
Plant	Creative, imaginative, unorthodox	Solves difficult problems
Monitor-evaluator	Sober, strategic, discerning	Sees all options; judges accurately
Shaper	Challenging, dynamic, enjoys pressure	Overcomes obstacles through drive
Coordinator	Mature, confident, good chair	Clarifies goals, promotes decision making, delegates
Resource investigator	Extrovert, enthusiastic, communicative	Explores opportunities; develops contacts
Team worker	Cooperative, mild, perceptive, tactical	Listens and builds; reduces conflict
Implementer	Disciplined, reliable, cooperative	Turns ideas into practical solutions
Completer finisher	Painstaking, conscientious, anxious	Searches out omissions; delivers on time
Specialist	Single minded, self-starting, dedicated	Provides scarce knowledge and skills
Comic	Unflappable, robust, resilient	Relieves tension

Table 2-13   Belbin's team roles and associated characteristics

Margerison and McCann

Margerison and McCann (1990) produced a leadership model based on two spectra:
- controlling behavior to exploring behavior
- advising roles to organizing roles.

The team roles adopted by an individual depend on the extent to which they apply these two fundamental behaviors. Nine team roles result, see Table 2-14. Many of these roles are similar to the roles identified by Belbin.

Myers-Briggs Type Indicator

The Myers-Briggs Type was developed by Briggs-Myers (1992), and mainly gives an indication of an individual's thinking style and temperament in a team. It describes the individual's personality on four scales:
- introversion to extroversion
- sensing to intuition
- thinking to feeling
- judgment to perception.

Team roles and leadership styles

It is a common fallacy to mix the team roles mentioned here with leadership styles, saying the team roles are styles adopted by leaders. Dulewicz and Higgs (2003) have shown that only some of the team roles and personality factors are correlated to performance as a leader.

	Exploring behavior preferred external orientation, developing options, divergent activities			
Advising roles Support roles required to get things done	Creator-innovator	Explorer-promoter	Assessor-developer	*Organizing roles* required to build and deliver product/service
	Reporter-adviser	Linker	Thruster-organizer	
	Upholder-maintainer	Controller-inspector	Concluder-producer	
	Controlling behavior preferred internal order, following plans, convergent work			

Table 2-14   Team roles identified by Margerison and McCann (1990)

1. *Belbin*: Dulewicz and Higgs (2003) showed that only the roles of resource investigator and team worker were strongly correlated to performance as a leader. The coordinator and implementer roles are weakly correlated to performance as a leader.
2. *16PF*: There was greater correlation of the 16PF personality factors with performance as a leader. The results suggest that extroverts and more emotionally stable individuals are likely to be better leaders. There is also some correlation with some of the other factors.

Based on these results, Dulewicz and Higgs (2003) suggest that their fifteen leader competencies give a better guidance to performance as a leader than Belbin roles or 16PF personality factors, though the latter are correlated to their fifteen leader competencies.

Personality and leadership

There is also substantial literature on the personality of leaders. As previously mentioned, Selmer (2002) suggests five personality traits. However, both the emotional intelligence and competency schools agree on this issue. It is the style, competence, or emotional intelligence that determines an individual's effectiveness as a leader. Leaders can mold and learn different styles for different circumstances. Their preferred style will be based on their personality. They can adapt their style and learn new ones, but they cannot change their personality.

Conclusion

We have seen a substantial amount of evidence that, in a general management context, different leadership styles are appropriate in different circumstances. Some writers have even suggested different leadership styles for different project contexts, and different project-like situations, such as the following:

- stage of the project life cycle
- complexity of change in organizations
- stage of the life cycle of a company
- stage of the product life cycle.

Considering this background, it would be extraordinary if the leadership style of the project manager did not influence project success, and different project leadership styles were not appropriate for different circumstances. So we look now at what the project management literature says about project success, and the contribution of the project manager to it.

Chapter 3

Project Success

The aim of this research was to determine whether the project manager's leadership style has an impact on project success, and whether different styles are better for different types of projects. To be able to answer these questions we need to know how we judge whether a project has been a success, and how we intend to categorize projects to know what we mean by different types of projects. We also should consider what has previously been said about the contribution of the project manager and his or her competence to project success. The literature on project success focuses on two areas, success factors and success criteria, as follows:

- Project success factors are those elements of the project and its management that can be influenced to increase the chance of a successful outcome.
- Project success criteria are the measures (both quantitative and qualitative) against which a project is judged to be successful.

In this chapter we consider the issue of project success. First, we look at what has been written about success factors over the last forty years, and particularly what has been written about the project manager, and his or her competence and leadership style, such as success factors. We then review the literature on project success to show how we will judge project success for our research model. Finally, we consider recent research into the categorization of projects, and say how we will judge project type in our research.

Project success factors

Jugdev and Müller (2005) described how our understanding of project success has changed over the last forty years. They identify four periods during which our view of what contributes to success has successively widened:

1. In the 1960s to 1970s, project success focused on the implementation stage, measuring time, cost, and functionality improvements.
2. In the 1980s and 1990s, the quality of the planning and hand-over was identified as important. Lists of critical success factors (CSF), which also took into account organizational and stakeholder perspectives, became popular.
3. More recently, new CSF frameworks have been developed on the basis that success is stakeholder-dependent and involves interaction between project supplier and recipient. Additional dimensions taken into account during this period have been: the project's product and its utilization; staff growth and development; the customer; benefits to the delivery organization; senior management; and the environment.
4. For the future, Jugdev and Müller anticipate a continuation in the broadening of the definition of success, especially taking into account factors from the conceptual stages of the project life cycle and the close-down of the project's product, together with an increasing understanding of the importance of the project sponsor's view of success.

We consider the second and third stages.

1980s and 1990s

The 1980s was a period of intense research into project success factors. Andersen et al. (1987) identified project pitfalls, things that project managers might do or not do, which increased the chance of failure. They identified pitfalls in the way the project is established, planned, organized, and controlled. The inverse of these are presented as success factors in Table 3-1. Morris (1988) identified both success factors and failure factors, again with different factors identified at successive stages of the project life cycle; see Table 3-2. Baker, Murphey, and Fisher (1988) also produced a list of project success factors; see Table 3-3. Pinto and Slevin (1988) in a now classic piece of work identified ten project success factors; see Table 3-4. This is now one of the most widely quoted lists. In Tables 3-2, 3-3, and 3-4, the factors are presented in order of decreasing impact. Unlike the others, Andersen et al. (1987) and Morris (1988) identified that different factors are appropriate at different stages of the project life cycle, suggesting different competencies are appropriate at

Project stage	Success factors
Foundation	Align the project with the business Gain commitment of involved managers Create a shared vision
Planning	Use multiple levels Use simple friendly tools Encourage creativity Estimate realistically
Implementation	Negotiate resource availability Agree cooperation Define management responsibility Gain commitment of resource providers Define channels of communication Project manager as manager not chief technologist
Control	Integrate plans and progress reports Formalize the review process through • defined intervals • defined criteria • controlled attendance Use sources of authority

Table 3-1   Project success factors after Andersen et al. (1987)

Stage	Success factors	Barriers
Formation	Personal ambition Top management support Team motivation Clear objectives Technological advantage	Unmotivated team Poor leadership Technical limitations Money
Build-up	Team motivation Personal motivation Top management support Technological expertise	Unmotivated team Conflict in objectives Poor leadership Poor top management support Technical problems
Execution	Team motivation Personal motivation Client support Top management support	Unmotivated team Poor top management support Deficient procedures
Close-out	Personal motivation Team motivation Top management support Financial support	Poor control Poor financial support Ill-defined objectives Poor leadership

Table 3-2   Project success factors after Morris (1988)

Success factors
Coordination and team-client relations
Adequacy of team structure and control
System uniqueness, importance, and public exposure
Success criteria salience and consensus
Competitive and budgetary pressure
Initial over-optimism and conceptual difficulty
Internal capabilities build-up

Table 3-3   Project success factors after Baker, Murphey, and Fisher (1988)

Success factor	Description
1. Project mission	Clearly defined goals and direction
2. Top management support	Resources, authority and power for implementation
3. Schedule and plans	Detailed specification of implementation process
4. Client consultation	Communication with and consultation of all stakeholders
5. Personnel	Recruitment, selection, and training of competent personnel
6. Technical tasks	Ability of the required technology and expertise
7. Client acceptance	Selling of the final product to the end users
8. Monitoring and feedback	Timely and comprehensive control
9. Communication	Provision of timely data to key players
10. Trouble-shooting	Ability to handle unexpected problems

Table 3-4   Project success factors after Pinto and Slevin (1988)

different stages. Morris mentioned leadership as a factor, and Andersen et al. mentioned the project manager's competence.

Pinto and Prescott (1988) suggested that personnel is not a success factor. Belout and Gauvreau (2004) questioned this result, because it is contrary to human resource management literature, but in their own study reached the same conclusion. However, both pairs of authors asked project managers what they thought was important. Because project managers tend to be task-oriented rather than people-oriented (Mäkilouko 2004) perhaps this result is predictable. To truly determine project success factors it may be necessary to measure what actually has an impact on project success. Andersen et al. (1987) determined their list from reviews of failed projects, so it was based on assessment of actual project performance.

Morris and Hough (1987) identified success factors from a study of seven major projects in the U.K. from the 1960s, 1970s, and 1980s. Some were successful, some unsuccessful. Morris (1997) further developed this list into a project strategy model, which Turner (1999) recast as the Seven Forces Model for project success (see Figure 3-1) with five success factors in each of seven areas: context, attitude, sponsorship, definition, people, systems, and organization.

2000s

There has recently been a revival of interest in project success factors. Hartman and Ashrafi (2002) identified a list of ten critical success factors for information systems projects, very similar to Pinto and Slevin's list. Cooke-Davies (2001) identified factors giving successful project management and factors leading to successful projects (see Table 3-5). Under successful project management, he identified six factors that help ensure a project is completed on time, and two more that help ensure it is completed within budget. He identified four more that help ensure the project is successful. His list was obtained from benchmarking project performance in several benchmarking networks he manages, so it is based on subjective assessment of actual project performance. Kendra and Taplin (2004) suggested a model of success factors grouped into four types: macro-social, micro-social, macro-technical and micro-technical. The leadership, behavior, and personal attributes of the project manager are proposed as one of the success factors in the micro-social list. Based on the quality model of the European Foundation for Quality Management, Westerveld and Gaya-Walters (2001) developed the Project Excellence Model (see Figure 3-2). This model combines both success factors and success criteria in one model. Success factors are shown on the left side of the model. Project leadership and project management are both shown as success factors.

Internal to Organization

Definition
- Objectives
- Scope
- Technology
- Design
- Resourcing

Systems
- Planning
- Control
- Reporting
- Quality
- Risk

People
- Leadership
- Management
- Teamwork
- Influence
- IR

Attitudes
- Commitment
- Motivation
- Support
- Right 1st Time
- Shared Vision

Pressures | **Project Drivers** | **Resistance**

Organization
- Roles
- Resources
- Type
- Contract Strategy

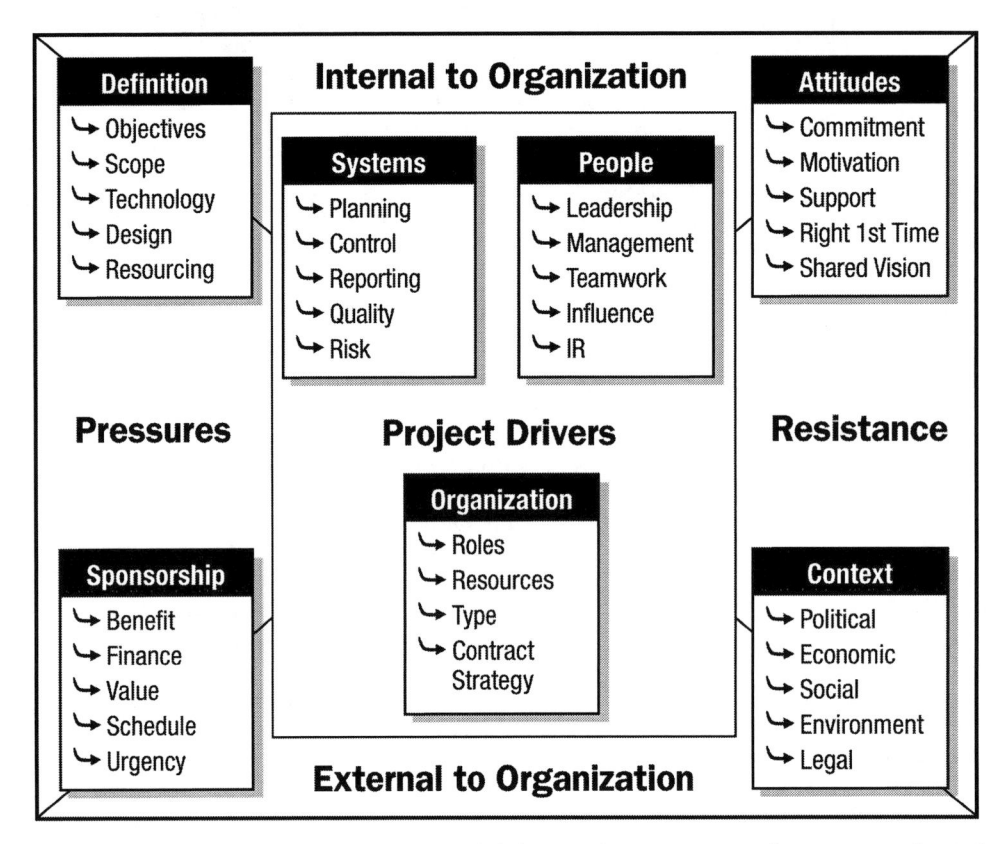

Sponsorship
- Benefit
- Finance
- Value
- Schedule
- Urgency

Context
- Political
- Economic
- Social
- Environment
- Legal

External to Organization

Figure 3-1   The Seven Forces Model for project success, after Turner (1999)

Project management success factors contributing to time completion:
F1   Adequacy of company-wide education on risk management
F2   Maturity of organization's processes for assigning ownership of risk
F3   Adequacy with which a visible risk register is maintained
F4   Adequacy of an up-to-date risk management plan
F5   Adequacy of documentation of organizational responsibilities on the project
F6   Project or stage duration as far below three years as possible, preferably below one year

Project management success factors contributing to budget completion:
F7   Changes to scope only made through a mature scope change control process
F8   Integrity of the performance measurement baseline

Additional project success factors contributing to successful benefits realization:
F9   Existence of an effective benefits delivery and management process that involves the mutual cooperation of project management and line management functions
F10 Portfolio and program management practices that allow the enterprise to resource fully a suite of projects that are thoughtfully and dynamically matched to the corporate strategy and business objectives
F11 A site of project, program, and portfolio management metrics that provide "direct line of sight" feedback on current project performance and anticipated future success, so that project, program, portfolio and corporate decisions can be aligned
F12 An effective means of learning from experience on projects that combine explicit knowledge with tacit knowledge in a way that encourages people to learn and to embed that learning into continuous improvement of project management processes and practices.

Table 3-5   Project success factors after Cooke-Davies (2001)

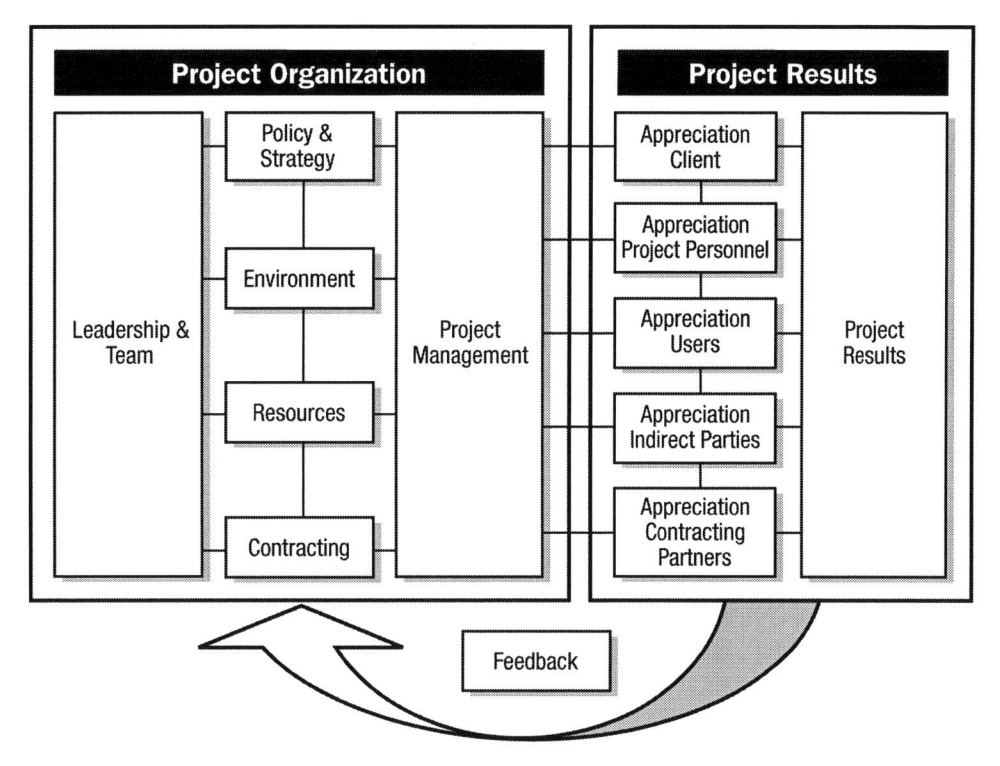

Figure 3-2   Project Excellence model, after Westerveld and Gaya-Walters (2001)

The project manager as a success factor

In the previous chapter we saw that in a general management context it has been shown that the manager's leadership style influences success, and different leadership styles are appropriate in different contexts. We saw that a very limited amount of research has been done to determine how the six schools of leadership can be applied in a project context, which is summarized in Table 3-6. We also saw that some of the authors have shown that in some project-like contexts certain leadership styles were appropriate. For instance:

School	Authors	Idea
Trait school	Turner (1999)	Seven traits of effective project leaders
Behavior school	Frame (1987), Turner (1999)	Four leadership behaviors: Laissez-faire, democratic, autocratic, bureaucratic
Contingency school	Frame (1987), Turner (1999)	Different behaviors at different stages of the life-cycle
Charismatic school	Keegan and Den Hartog (2004)	No preference on projects for transformational or transactional leadership
Emotional intelligence school	Lee-Kelley, Leong, and Loong (2003)	Perception of success depends on the managers emotional intelligence
Competence school	Crawford (2001, 2005) Dainty, Cjeng, and Moore (2005)	Different competence profiles for different projects Twelve behavioral competencies associated with construction project management

Table 3-6   Project leadership and the schools of leadership

- Goleman, Boyatzis, and McKee (2002) suggested that two styles that they describe as "toxic," pacesetting, and commanding are appropriate in turnaround situations, but not in more routine management situations.
- Dulewicz and Higgs (2003) showed that three leadership styles: goal-oriented, involving, and engaging, were appropriate on change projects with different levels of change—normal, complex, and transformational, respectively.
- Clarke and Pratt (1985), Rodrigues (1988), and Slevin (1989) showed that different leadership styles are appropriate at different stages of the cycle of growth and operation of a business.

In stark contrast, a notable absence from many of the lists of success factors presented is any mention of the project manager. The manager, his or her competence, personality, or leadership style is hardly ever mentioned as a success factor for projects. Many of the lists imply that the project needs to be well managed, and name specific management functions that need to be well done, and so imply that the project manager needs to be competent, but they do not mention the project manager directly.

Baker, Murphy, and Fisher (1988) (Table 3-2), Pinto and Slevin (1988) (Table 3-4), and Cooke-Davies (2001) (Table 3-5), do not mention the project manager at all. Andersen et al. (1987) (Table 3-1) say the manager should be chosen for his or her management skill, and not design expertise. Morris (1988) (Table 3-2) shows poor leadership as a barrier to success. Turner (1999) in his Seven Forces Model (Figure 3-1) shows leadership and management as success factors, and Westerveld and Gaya-Walters (2001) in their Project Excellence Model (Figure 3-2), show leadership as a success factor. Kendra and Taplin (2004) directly suggest the project manager's leadership style and competence as a potential success factor for projects. However, the project management literature is quite reticent at mentioning the project manager, and his or her competence and leadership style, as a success factor for projects. However, the silence has not been deafening; some work has been done over the years. For instance, authors have suggested the following:

1. The project manager's competence is related to their success as a project manager.
2. Different project leadership styles are appropriate at each stage of the project life cycle
3. Specific leadership styles are appropriate for multicultural projects.
4. Project managers have a leadership role in creating an effective working environment for the project team.
5. Project managers prefer task-oriented to people-oriented leadership styles.
6. The project manager's leadership style influences his or her perception of success.

Competence and success

The most significant work on correlating the project manager's competence to his or her success was done by Crawford (2001). Crawford's measure of success was not project performance, but assessment by the supervisor, so it was a subjective assessment by the line manager. Further it was an assessment of overall performance, not on a specific project. Crawford found that once a project manager has achieved an entry level of knowledge, more knowledge does not make them more competent. However, improvement in the other dimensions of competence, skills, and personal characteristics, can make them more competent. This was confirmed by work of Hobbs, Petteren, and Guérette (2004) and Besner and Hobbs (2004).

Management style through the life cycle

Frame (1987) was the first to suggest that different leadership styles are appropriate at different stages of the project life cycle. Building on his work, Turner (1999) suggested four leadership styles based on how much the project manager involves the team in decision-making, decision-taking, and his or her flexibility (refer to Table 2-3). He then suggested different styles were appropriate at each stage of the life cycle (refer to Table 2-4). Turner (1999) also considered different cultural styles, using Hofstede's (1991) four cultural parameters (refer to Table 2-8): power distance; uncertainty avoidance; individuality vs. collectivism; masculinity vs. femininity. He showed that different combinations of the four parameters were appropriate at different stages of the life cycle.

Multicultural projects

Many authors have written about the leadership styles appropriate on multicultural projects (for instance, see Hofstede 1991; Trompenaars 1993; Björkman and Schaap 1992; Hastings and Briner 1996; Turner 1999; Selmer 2002; Rees 2003; Mäkilouko 2004). Björkman and Schaap (1992) say expatriate managers adopt one of three styles:
- Didactical: they sell ideas by analogy and site visits.

- Organization design: they carefully choose team members to design conflict out.
- Culturally blind: they do not recognize cultural differences.

Selmer (2002) suggests personality traits for coping with cultural differences:
- agreeableness
- conscientiousness
- emotional stability
- intellect
- openness/extroversion.

Mäkilouko (2004) suggests most project managers adopt task-oriented styles that are inappropriate in multicultural situations, but suggest some project managers adopt two other more appropriate styles:
- people-oriented
- relationship-oriented.

Team fusion

Thamhain (2004) showed the working environment within the project team has a significant impact on project success, and therefore suggests that the project manager has a significant leadership role in fusing the team. Kloppenborg and Petrick (1999) suggested that project leaders have a role in developing team characteristics into a collective set of virtues including the following:
- ethics and honesty
- respect and trust for others
- prudence
- courage
- responsible use and sharing of power.

Turner and Müller (2003) made similar suggestions when they compared the project manager to the chief executive of the temporary organization that is the project, and so suggested he or she should adopt Barnard's (1938) cognitive and cathectic styles.

Task versus people focus

In the last chapter we saw that a task versus leadership focus has been a recurring theme in the leadership literature (see Fiedler 1967). Mäkilouko (2004) showed that project managers are mainly task-focused, with 40 out of 47 project managers in his sample being purely task-focused. On the other hand, Lee-Kelley, Leong, and Loong (2003) found half their sample was relationship-oriented. Keegan and Den Hartog (2004) predicted that a project manager's leadership style needs to be more transformational than transactional, but found no significant link. Whereas for line managers there is a significant correlation between the manager's leadership style and staff commitment, motivation, and stress, there was no such correlation for project managers.

Leadership style and perception of success

Lee-Kelley, Leong, and Loong (2003) set out to find which project management knowledge areas are critical to project success and whether the project manager's leadership style influences his or her perception of control. What they found was the project manager's leadership style influenced his or her perception of success on the project.

Project success criteria

We now need to consider how we are going to judge project success. Wateridge (1995) identified that up to the early 1990s most of the work on project success had been on success factors. But he suggested that before you could determine appropriate success factors for a project you had to know how it would be judged to be successful. Morris and Hough (1987) through their research into major projects identified a list of success criteria for projects:
- the project delivers its functionality
- it is on time, to cost, and to quality
- it is profitable to the contractor
- if necessary, it is terminated promptly.

Wateridge developed his own list of success criteria and showed what success factors would help deliver these success criteria (Table 3-7). Turner (2004) combined these two models into a list of success criteria. He also identified that different stakeholders would be interested in each criterion and that they would make their judgments at different times (Table 3-8). He suggested that what would lead to the best outcome for a

Success Factors	Success Criteria							
	Commercial success	Meets user requirements	Meets budget	Happy users	Achieves purpose	Meets timescales	Happy sponsor	Meets quality	Happy team
Leadership				Secondary			Secondary		Primary
Motivation				Secondary					Primary
Planning	Primary	Secondary	Primary	Secondary	Secondary	Primary	Secondary	Secondary	Secondary
Monitoring	Primary		Primary			Primary			Secondary
Development method	Primary	Secondary						Primary	
Management method									Primary
Delegation				Secondary					Primary
Communication		Primary		Primary			Primary		
Clear goals	Secondary	Primary			Primary			Secondary	
User involvement	Secondary	Primary		Primary	Primary		Primary	Primary	
Top management	Primary		Primary			Primary	Primary		

Key: Primary: primary success factor influencing this criterion
Secondary: secondary success factor influencing this criterion

Table 3-7   Success criteria and associated success factors after Wateridge (1995)

Success Criteria	Interested Stakeholders	Timescale
Increases shareholder value	Shareholders, sponsor	End + years
Makes a profit for the owner	Owner	End + years
Satisfies owner and sponsor	Sponsor, owner	End + years
Satisfies consumers	Consumers	End + years
Satisfies users and champion	Users, champion	End + years
Achieves purpose	Users, champion, owner	End + months
Meets specification • Functionality • Flexibility, reliability, availability, maintainability, elasticity, security	Users, champion, team	End + weeks
Time, cost, quality	Project team, users	End
Satisfies project team	Project team	End
Makes a profit for the contractor	Project team	End

Table 3-8   Project success criteria, interested stakeholders, and timescales over which they make their judgment, after Turner (2004)

project was to negotiate a balanced view of success among all the stakeholders. Because projects are coupled nonlinear systems, to optimize the project for one stakeholder at the expense of the others would not lead to a successful outcome. This was confirmed by Müller (Turner and Müller 2004) who showed that cooperation between the project manager and project sponsor is a necessary condition for project success.

In our research we initially chose to use the five parameters for project success suggested by Westerveld and Gaya-Walters (2001) in the right side of their model:
1. Appreciation of the client
2. Appreciation of the users
3. Appreciation of the project team
4. Appreciation of contracting partners
5. Appreciation of other stakeholders.

However, as we shall see in the next chapter, we extended this list as a result of the interviews that we conducted.

The project management literature on project categorization

Crawford, Hobbs, and Turner (2005) produced the definitive report on the categorization of projects. Through their research project they reviewed the literature on categorization systems and prior work on the categorization of projects. They then interviewed several companies from three continents on the categorization systems they adopted. From this they developed a model for the categorization of projects, which they tested through a web-based questionnaire. They then revised their model and validated it with the companies they originally interviewed. They showed that in common with most categorization systems, project categorization systems have two main elements:
- the purposes for which project are categorized
- the attributes used to categorize projects.

Most organizations have two main reasons for categorizing projects (see Figure 3-3).
1. To align projects with strategic intent, and to prioritize projects for assigning resources
2. To assign and develop appropriate capabilities to manage those projects selected.

The two main purposes are to do the correct projects, and to do the chosen projects correctly. Crawford, Hobbs, and Turner (2005) identified a number of subsidiary purposes (Figure 3-3). Interestingly, although they identified choosing a project manager of the right skills as one subsidiary purpose, they did not identify choosing a project manager of the appropriate personality. However, they did not claim that their list of purposes was comprehensive.

Figure 3-3: Categorization of Projects in Organizations

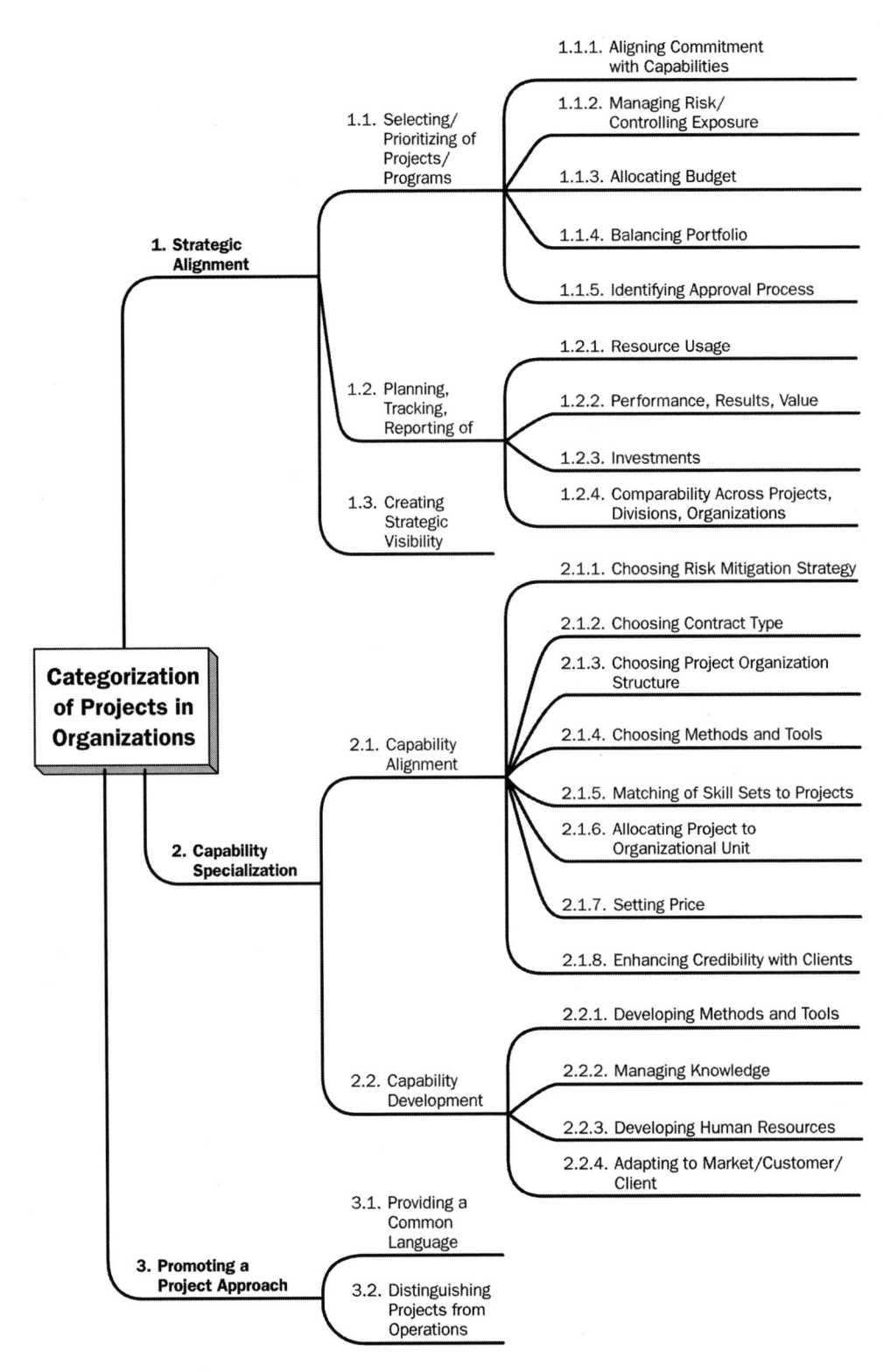

1. Strategic Alignment
- 1.1. Selecting/Prioritizing of Projects/Programs
  - 1.1.1. Aligning Commitment with Capabilities
  - 1.1.2. Managing Risk/Controlling Exposure
  - 1.1.3. Allocating Budget
  - 1.1.4. Balancing Portfolio
  - 1.1.5. Identifying Approval Process
- 1.2. Planning, Tracking, Reporting of
  - 1.2.1. Resource Usage
  - 1.2.2. Performance, Results, Value
  - 1.2.3. Investments
  - 1.2.4. Comparability Across Projects, Divisions, Organizations
- 1.3. Creating Strategic Visibility

2. Capability Specialization
- 2.1. Capability Alignment
  - 2.1.1. Choosing Risk Mitigation Strategy
  - 2.1.2. Choosing Contract Type
  - 2.1.3. Choosing Project Organization Structure
  - 2.1.4. Choosing Methods and Tools
  - 2.1.5. Matching of Skill Sets to Projects
  - 2.1.6. Allocating Project to Organizational Unit
  - 2.1.7. Setting Price
  - 2.1.8. Enhancing Credibility with Clients
- 2.2. Capability Development
  - 2.2.1. Developing Methods and Tools
  - 2.2.2. Managing Knowledge
  - 2.2.3. Developing Human Resources
  - 2.2.4. Adapting to Market/Customer/Client

3. Promoting a Project Approach
- 3.1. Providing a Common Language
- 3.2. Distinguishing Projects from Operations

Figure 3-3   Reasons for categorizing projects, after Crawford, Hobbs, and Turner (2005)

Crawford, Hobbs, and Turner (2005) identified an extensive list of attributes used for categorizing projects. They realized that the potential list was without end, but they found they could group their attributes used into fourteen groups, and that these covered all the categorization systems they encountered in their literature review and field work (Figure 3-4). Within each of these fourteen groupings there was potentially a limitless

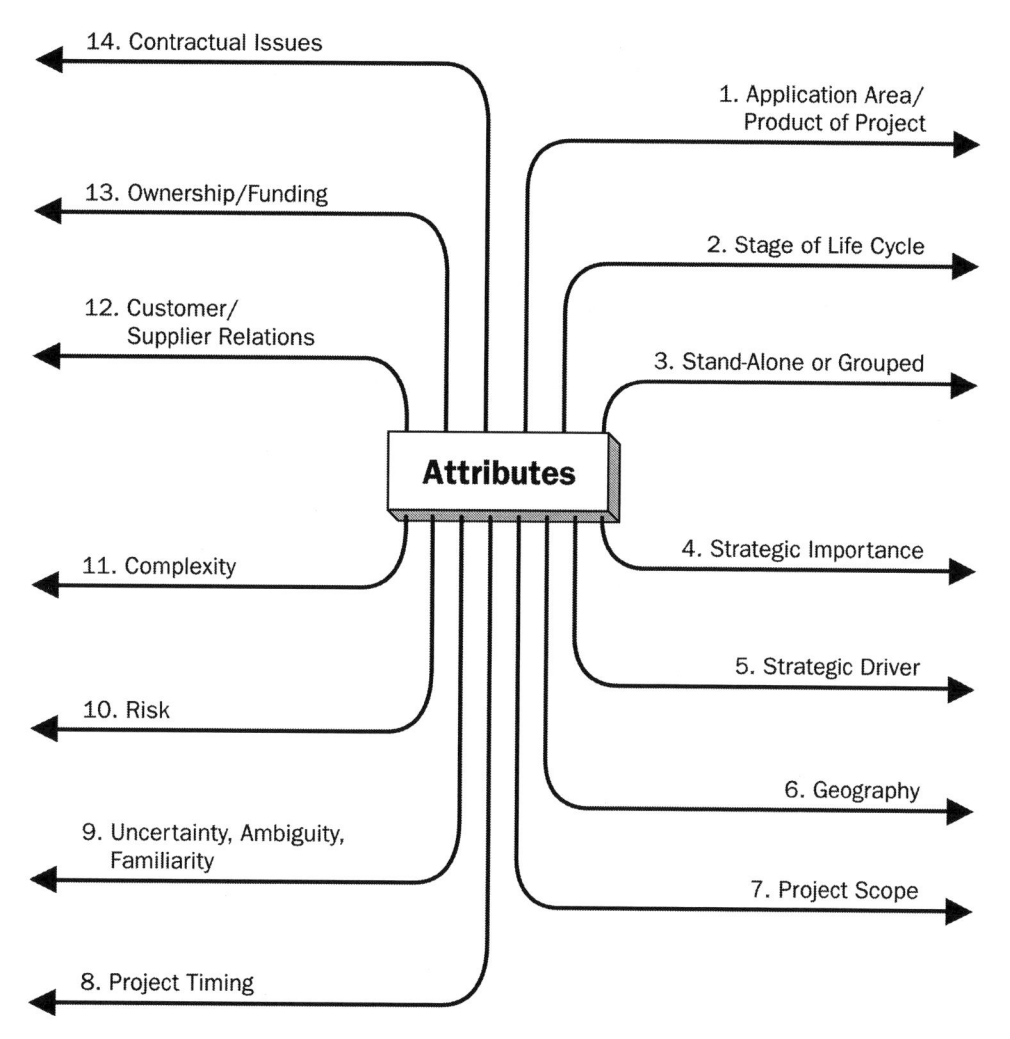

Figure 3-4   Groups of attributes for categorizing projects, after Crawford, Hobbs, and Turner (2005)

number of ways to categorize projects, dependent on the need of the user organization. They also showed that even more complex systems of categorization could be envisaged by creating combinations or hierarchies of attributes. However, they were able to suggest common models of categorization systems used. Appendix C gives one, two, or three highly simplified models under each of the fourteen attribute groupings.

For our research model, using fourteen attribute groupings would be too complex. It would not be possible to test the impact of that many project types on project success without gathering substantial data. We therefore decided initially to limit ourselves to five attribute groupings and two, three, or four project types under each grouping giving us sixteen project types. However, as a result of our interviews we found we needed to add a sixth attribute, form of contract, giving nineteen project types in all (Table 3-9). Although this is clearly a simplification, it is necessary to make progress. It has enabled us to demonstrate the impact of project type on the link between project manager personality type and project success, because such a link exists for these nineteen project types. If we had not found such an impact for any of these nineteen project types, it would not have meant that such a link did not exist for other project types, but we achieved a positive result for the categories we adopted.

Other authors have already suggested or demonstrated a relationship between project manager personality type and project success under some of these project types, and that gives us some confidence that limiting ourselves to these six attribute groupings and these nineteen project types will enable us to make progress.

Project attribute	Project types by attribute
Application area	Engineering and construction ICT Business
Complexity	High Medium Low
Life-cycle stage	Feasibility Design Execution Close-out
Strategic importance	Mandatory Repositioning Renewal
Culture	Domestic Host Ex-patriot
Form of contract	Fixed price Remeasurement Alliance

Table 3-9   A simplified model for project categories

(a) Frame (1987) suggests that different leadership styles are necessary at different stages of the project life cycle.
(b) Turner (1999) also suggests that different cultural styles are necessary at different stages of the project life cycle.
(c) Dulewicz and Higgs (2003) show that different leadership styles are necessary depending on the complexity of change projects.
(d) Shenhar (2001) suggests different leadership styles are appropriate for technological projects of differing complexity.
(e) Mäkilouko (2004) shows specific leadership styles are needed on multicultural projects.
(f) Partington (1997) describes a case in which an engineering and construction company used two of its best project managers from the field to manage an internal change project, but they did not find themselves well suited to that new role.

Chapter 4

Research Methodology

Aims and approach

The ultimate aim of our research is to develop a framework to help the managers of project managers select an appropriate project manager for a given project based on his or her leadership style. To achieve that we set two aims for this research project, to show the following:
1. The project manager's competence, including his or her leadership style, influences project success.
2. Different competence profiles, including different leadership styles, are appropriate for different types of projects.

To achieve this, our research has been conducted in six stages:

Stage 1: Undertake a literature review
Stage 2: Develop a research model based on the literature review
Stage 3: Conduct qualitative, semi-structured interviews to test and revise the research model
Stage 4: Conduct a quantitative Web-based questionnaire
Stage 5: Validate the results of the Web-based questionnaire with the interviewees
Stage 6: Develop profiles of project managers best suitable for different types of projects

The literature review is described in the previous chapter. Based on the literature search we have formulated the following hypotheses:

Hypothesis 1: The project manager's competency, which includes his or her leadership style, is positively correlated to project success.
Hypothesis 2: Different combinations of project management competency are correlated with success on different types of projects.

Research model

Our research model is shown in Figure 4-1.

Independent variable

The independent variable is project management competence, particularly leadership style. The leadership competencies we have chosen to use to test Hypotheses 1 and 2 are the fifteen competencies identified by Dulewicz and Higgs (2003), listed in Table 2-6 and repeated in Table 4-1 for convenience. Dulewicz and Higgs's definitions of their fifteen competencies are given in Appendix B.

Dependent variable

The dependent variable is project success. We originally chose to use the five success criteria suggested by Westerveld and Gaya-Walters (2001) (see Figure 3-2):
- appreciation of the sponsor
- appreciation of the users
- appreciation of the suppliers
- appreciation of the project team
- appreciation of the other stakeholders.

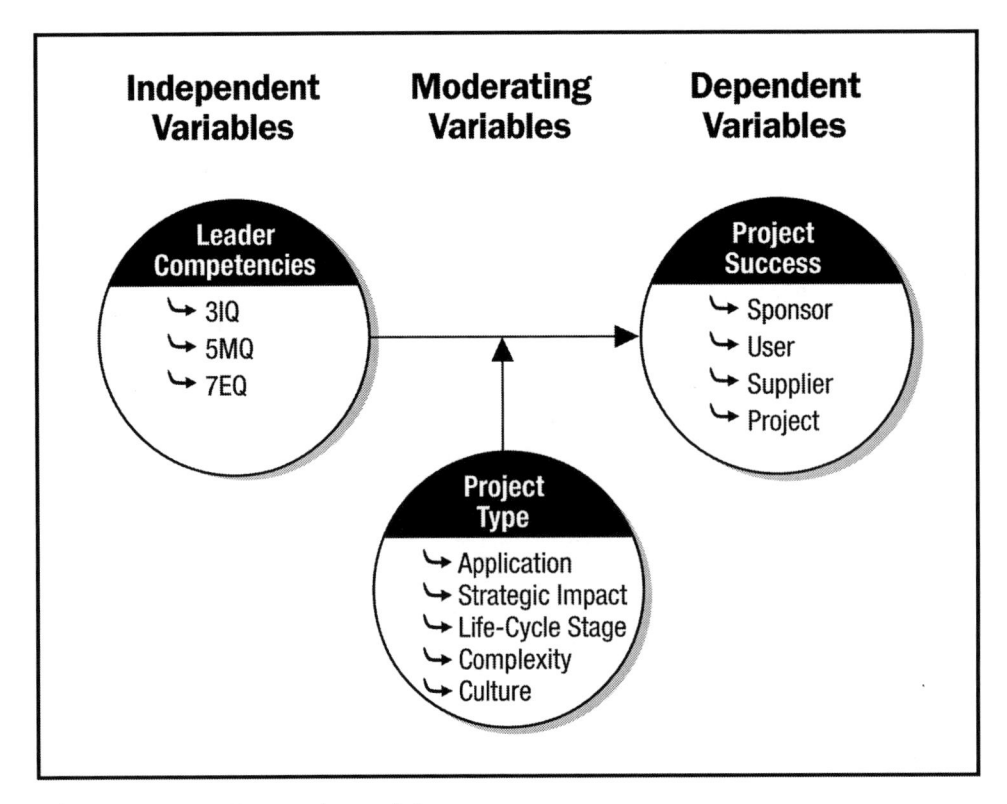

Figure 4-1   Research model

Group	Competency
Intellectual (IQ)	critical analysis and judgment vision and imagination strategic perspective
Managerial (MQ)	engaging communication managing resources empowering developing achieving
Emotional (EQ)	self-awareness emotional resilience motivation sensitivity influence intuitiveness conscientiousness

Table 4-1   Fifteen leadership competencies, after Dulewicz and Higgs (2003)

However, based on the results of the interviews, we decided to extend the list to ten criteria, as shown in Table 4-2. We will describe the reasons for this in the next chapter. We accept that these definitions of project success are not comprehensive and are more qualitative and therefore more subjective in nature. However, if we achieve a positive result with these definitions of success criteria, then the hypotheses will be supported. If we had achieved a null result, the hypotheses would not be disproved because they might be valid against other measures of project success.

Success criteria
Meeting project's overall performance (functionality, budget, and timing)
Meeting user requirements
Meeting the project's purpose
Client satisfaction with the project results
Reoccurring business with the client
End-user satisfaction with the project's product or service
Suppliers' satisfaction
Project team's satisfaction
Other stakeholders' satisfaction
Meeting the respondent's self-defined success factor

Table 4-2   Success criteria used for this study

Moderating variable

Project type is a moderating variable for Hypothesis 2. It means that project type influences the strength and nature of the relationship between project manager leadership style and project success. Crawford, Hobbs, and Turner (2005) suggested fourteen attributes for categorizing projects. However, we do not feel able to encompass all attribute types in our research model, so we initially chose to focus on just five, with sixteen associated types of project, as shown in Table 3-9. As a result of our interviews we decided to add a sixth attribute, contract types, with three further types of projects (see Table 4-3). The reason for this is described in the next chapter. Thus, our research model is not comprehensive, but if we achieve a positive result for these nineteen types of projects, then we can say the following:
- The project manager's leadership style influences project success
- Different styles are appropriate for different types of project

If we had achieved a null result, the hypotheses would not be disproved because they might be valid against other measures of project success.

Project attribute	Project types by attribute	Example authors
Application area	Engineering and construction ICT Business	Crawford (2001, 2005)
Complexity	High Medium Low	Dulewicz and Higgs (2003)
Life-cycle stage	Feasibility Design Execution Close-out	Turner (1999) Frame (1987)
Strategic importance	Mandatory Repositioning Renewal	
Culture	Single culture Host Expatriate	Rees (2003)
Contract type	Fixed price Remeasurement Alliance	Turner (2004)

Table 4-3   Final model for project categorization used in the research

Interviews

Initially, we undertook a qualitative study by conducting fourteen semi-structured interviews with project managers and line managers responsible for assigning project managers to projects. The objective of the interviews was to identify factors applied by managers for selecting project managers for different project types, and to test the relevance of our research model before conducting the Web-based questionnaire. The structure of the interviews is shown in Appendix D and the results in Appendix E.

Nature of the company

We first asked the interviewees questions about the nature of the company and the projects undertaken. We asked the following:

1. What sort of business the company undertakes. We sought interviewees from a range of companies, some doing internal development projects for themselves, some doing projects for others. Of those doing projects for others some were managing other people's projects and some providing works or services (including consultancy).
2. We were interested in the management philosophy of the company because we thought it might influence their choice of project managers.
3. We wanted to know the size and number of projects undertaken. Again, we sought a range of different sizes of company, some undertaking small projects, and some undertaking larger projects. Most of the organizations had a substantial project portfolio and so were repeatedly involved in choosing project managers.
4. We asked what types of project they undertook and asked them to categorize them against the five attributes and sixteen project types of projects we had chosen from our literature review (see Table 3-9). (There were only five attributes at this point.) We first asked them to describe the types of project they did to allow them to suggest alternatives to our model, but then wished to confirm the validity of our model.
5. Out of interest, we also asked the interviewees to rate the project management maturity of their organizations. This may have influenced the choice of project manager.

Project success

We needed to understand how the interviewees judged project success, to test the validity of our model. As previously discussed, as a result of the interviews we changed our method of judging project success from five criteria to ten (Table 4-2). We also asked whether they thought their view of project success influenced the choice of project manager.

Project manager's personality style and type of project

The main focus of the interviews was whether organizations consider the project manager's leadership style when selecting project managers for projects. We asked a range of questions:

1. We asked the interviewees whether they thought their project managers were more task- or people-focused. This had been identified in the literature survey as a significant difference in leadership styles, the difference between transactional or transformational leaders, whether they focus on people or process.
2. If project managers in an organization tended to veer toward one extreme or another we were interested in whether the interviewee might have a view as to why this might be.
3. We also wanted to know whether they thought it was appropriate.
4. We asked the interviewees what they thought were important personality characteristics or leadership styles for project managers. We wanted their views before showing the competency profile we had chosen from our literature search.
5. We asked whether they had a view on what the important competencies might be.
6. Then we asked them to rate the importance of the competencies from the competency profile we had chosen to use from our literature search (see Table 4-1) as high medium or low.

Selecting project managers

We then wanted to know whether project type is a factor taken into account when selecting project managers. We wanted to know the following:

1. What types of project the interviewees companies undertook.
2. Whether they look for different types of project managers on different types of projects.
3. Whether they thought other dimensions were important.

Other issues

We gave the interviewees an opportunity to volunteer other ideas they thought were important.

After analysis of the interviews we developed the first tentative theory about the importance of different leadership styles in different types of projects. This is reported in Chapter 5. The interviews also served as a check for the validity of the research model, prior to our launch of the worldwide, Web-based survey on project type, project success, and leadership style in projects. The data collected were subsequently used for statistical tests of the hypotheses.

Web-based questionnaire

Following the interviews we conducted a worldwide, Web-based questionnaire.

Questions

The questionnaire had two parts, each with two sets of questions. The first two sets of questions from part one are shown in Appendix F. We are not able to include part two, the second two sets of questions, because it is proprietary to Henley Management College.

Project type questions: This was assessed by using the nineteen project attributes and types shown in Table 4-3. Respondents were asked to select one or several project types within each project attribute category.

Project success questions: Based on the input we received in the interviews (see Chapter 5), we extended the definition of project success to ten factors (see Table 4-3). We asked the respondents to rate the ten criteria in judging the success of their projects as the following:

- not important at all
- not important
- slightly important
- important
- very important.

We then asked them to judge the success of their last project against the ten dimensions on a 5-point Likert scale from "Disagree" to "Agree."

Leadership questions: This part of the questionnaire contained 189 questions on the fifteen competency dimensions shown in Table 4-1. A 5-point Likert scale from "Never" to "Always" was used to identify respondents' behavior in respect to the fifteen competency dimensions, and its organizational context. This part of the questionnaire was originally developed by Dulewicz and Higgs (2003). To use the questions we bought a license from Henley Management College, U.K. and were supported by Vic Dulewicz and Malcolm Higgs for the analysis of this part of the questionnaire.

Demographic questions: Demographics on the respondent's job function, education, nationality, age, gender, and project management certification were captured. Respondents' e-mail address was asked from those interested in receiving a summary of the research results.

The first two sets of questions, on project type and project success, were asked on a Web site of Umeå University using their local tool for Web surveys. At the end of those two sets of questions, a link was provided to the leadership-style questionnaire, which is hosted by Henley Management College, U.K. Reconciliation of the answers to the two sets of questionnaires was done using the name of the respondents and the timestamps of their entries.

Questionnaire pilot

The questionnaire was piloted over a period of two weeks using twenty-one respondents. A minor change to the wording was made after three days in the pilot. No further changes were made for the official launch of the questionnaire. The five responses collected prior to the changes made on day three of the pilot were not used for the final analysis. All other responses were used in the analysis of the questionnaire.

Questionnaire launch

To ensure quality in responses, the aim was to make the questionnaire global, sending it to professionals in project management worldwide. Therefore, members of professional organizations in project management were targeted as respondents. An introduction e-mail, together with a Web link to the online questionnaire were sent to presidents of PMI chapters and special interest groups, as well as to all country representatives of IPMA (International Project Management Association), and the presidents of APM (Association of Project Management) and ASAPM (American Society for the Advancement of Project Management). The questionnaire was also sent to masters students on project management programs at universities in the U.K., Ireland, Australia, New Zealand, U.S., and Canada.

The introduction e-mail explained the purpose and time frame of the research and asked the receivers to forward this e-mail to their organization's members, for them to answer the questionnaire. The sampling frame consisted therefore of the approximately 300,000 members of these professional organizations and universities. The snowball approach to sampling, however, did not allow controlling how many of these members received the questionnaire.

Questionnaire analysis

The questionnaire was held open for four weeks. Subsequent analysis was done by identifying the nature of the relationship between different leadership styles and project success, and how this is influenced by project type. This was done using quantitative multivariate techniques, such as multivariate regression analysis. Through that, we tested Hypotheses 1 and 2. Furthermore, we analyzed the importance of the three competences and their fifteen competency dimensions for project success in different project types. The results where structured by performance levels of projects. Comparing results from high-performing projects with results from projects with other performance levels allowed for identification of those leadership dimensions that are correlated with success in different types of projects—and, therefore, critical for project success. Through that, those project manager competencies with the highest impact on success were identified for different types of projects. The data from the Web-based questionnaire are presented in Appendix G and the results in Chapter 6.

Validation

For the development of a final model we compared the results of the quantitative study (Web-based questionnaire) with the results of the qualitative study (interviews) in order to identify overlapping results. Similar results in both studies were considered to be validated results. This approach of results triangulation is often used in multi-method studies to achieve highest levels of credibility for the overall results. Validation was done through a reconciliation of the following:
- the "managers view," which was captured through the interviews, and
- the reality applied in projects, which was captured through the Web-based, global questionnaire.

We used the ranking results of the fifteen dimensions from the interviews, and compared these with the findings from the questionnaire analysis. The rankings from the interviews were grouped by project type (engineering and construction, information technology, and organizational change) and the average ranking of the fifteen dimensions calculated for each project type. Values up to 2.0 were considered low, 2.1 to 2.5 medium, and greater than 2.5 high. That gave the particular rankings of the importance of each of the fifteen competence dimensions (by the interviewees) for all projects and for each project type.

These rankings were subsequently compared with the results from the quantitative analysis. A match of interview rating being medium or high from the qualitative study, with a dimension that was found to be statistically significantly related with project performance (through the quantitative study) was then considered a validated result because of its appearance within both studies. Those dimensions that were found negatively related with project results in the quantitative study were checked for being ranked "low" in the qualitative study. Such a match was also considered a validated result. The triangulation results are further described in Chapter 6.

Project manager profiles

Finally, after having determined the importance of the EQ, MQ, and IQ competences, and associated fifteen competency dimensions to project success, we sought to determine the extent these dimensions were present in the managers of high performing projects. That allowed us developing project manager profiles for each individual project type. This was done in several steps:
1. We identified those dimensions that are stronger in high performing projects.
2. We then identified those dimensions that are stronger in different types of projects. For example, are project managers in highly complex project more motivational than their peers in medium complexity projects?

3. The measures of the fifteen dimensions were normalized and the sample compared to a control group.
4. We could then categorize each respondent's score against each of the fifteen competencies as high, medium, or low by comparison to the control group.
5. We could then identify the profile of the managers of high performing projects for most of the project types, categorizing them as high, medium, or low against each of the fifteen dimensions.

By this method, we were able to identify the following:
- the fifteen competency dimensions important for high project performance in different project types
- the extent to which of each of those dimensions is required for high project performance in different project types.

The method of analysis is described in detail in Appendix G, and the results in Chapter 7.

CHAPTER 5

Interviews

We undertook a qualitative study by conducting fourteen semi-structured interviews with senior project managers and line managers responsible for assigning project managers to projects. The objective of the interviews was to identify factors applied by managers for selecting project managers for different project types, and to test the relevance of our research model before conducting the Web-based questionnaire. The structure of the interviews is shown in Appendix D, and the reasoning behind that structure is described in Chapter 4. In this chapter we describe the results of the interviews. Data from the interviews is given in Appendix E.

Companies interviewed

We interviewed fourteen people from several companies. Information about the companies is given in Table E-1 of Appendix E. We have included information about ownership of the company. That was not a question asked, but was identified by some interviewees as significant in their selection of project managers. Particularly, three from privately owned companies said that maintaining long-term relationships with customers was more important than year-on-year profit growth, and that required a different type of project manager. To improve generalizability of the results we interviewed people from eight countries (see Table 5-1) and several industries (see Table 5-2). Some organizations were doing their own internal projects (back office) and some projects for others (front office). Of those doing projects for others, some were managing other organizational projects (body-shopping project managers), and others were providing goods and services. In Table 5-2 we have separated project management consultancy services from other services such as design. The firms ranged in size from 50 personnel to 10,000. Projects ranged in size from €50,000 to €500 million. We asked the interviewees to make an assessment of the project management maturity of their company to see if maturity made a difference. All rated their companies medium to high, but from the interviews, maturity seemed to have no impact on the selection of project managers.

Countries	Interviews
Austria	three
Australia	one
France	two
Germany	one
Sweden	four
The Netherlands	one
U.K.	one
U.S.	one

Table 5-1   Countries from which the interviewees came

Type	Service	Nature of firm	Number
Front office	Project management personnel	Project management consultants	five
Front office	Works or services to others	Information systems Research and development Mechanical and design contractor	four one one
Front office	Management consultancy	Project management consultants	six
Back office	Managing internal projects	Telecommunications Manufacturing Aerospace	four one one

Table 5-2   Industries from which the interviewees came

Types of projects

The nature of projects undertaken by the interviewees' companies is listed in Table E-2 of Appendix E. All of the organizations interviewed could identify with at least some of the types of projects listed in Table 3-3, and said that some of these attributes were important in choosing the leadership style of the project manager. When initially asked the types of project they undertook, some interviewees said they undertook other types from the fourteen attribute areas identified by Crawford, Hobbs, and Turner (2005). Table E-3 of Appendix E shows the attributes and project types undertaken by the interviewees' companies against the attributes and types of projects in Table 3-3.

Application area

All firms undertook projects from at least one application area from Table 3-3, and some undertook two areas. Two firms undertook projects from all three application areas. Some companies undertaking projects from two or more application areas said the project manager's competence was a criterion for assigning the project manager to a project. Most considered the project manager's technical knowledge and experience were important, but some also mentioned leadership style. For example, one interviewee from a telecommunications company said her organization undertook information systems and business change projects. Project managers for information systems projects should be technically competent and task-focused. But leadership skills are significant for organizational change projects. On those projects, the manager must be able to communicate with stakeholders, and deal with his or her emotions, particularly fear, aggression, and conflict. He or she must also be able to deal with ambiguity. The project manager must be self-confident, stable, and tolerant (the doctrine of the mean).

Success criteria mentioned	Times
Client satisfaction	5 times
Repeat business	5 times
Stakeholder satisfaction	4 times
Objectives met	5 times
Project value	1 time
Functionality, quality met	3 times
Cost met	4 times
Time met	4 times
Safety	1 time
Respond to problems	2 times
Project prioritized so resources available	1 time

Table 5-3   Success criteria and number of times mentioned

Complexity

Only seven interviewees defined what they meant by complexity, and it differed from firm to firm. Criteria for defining complexity included: size of project, number of departments involved, number and type of stakeholders, location of the project, and form of contract. Many interviewees identifying complexity said the project manager's leadership style was an issue when choosing the manager for complex projects, but not for simple projects. Two said they would carefully consider the leadership style of the manager for projects in Nigeria, but not other geographies, including other African countries. One also said leadership style was important when choosing the manager for a brown-field, retrofit project with a remeasurement contract, but not for a green-field project with a fixed-price contract. The interviewee above said she would consider leadership style for organizational change projects but not information systems projects. The managing director of project management consultancy described one project that had a significant environmental impact. He assigned two project managers. One to communicate with the outside world, particularly the environmental lobby, and another to communicate with project resources, mainly academics who were providing the science. He considered these required two different leadership skills.

Life-cycle stage

All organizations undertook projects from several stages of the project management life cycle, but few interviewees said the stage of the life cycle was a significant factor in choosing the project manager. One, working on information systems projects in the telecommunication company previously mentioned, said the concept, feasibility, and implementation stages would be managed by somebody from the business and the design stage by somebody from the information systems department. The main reason he gave was that design required technical knowledge, whereas the other stages required business knowledge. But his colleague stated that in implementation, the management of stakeholders is significant, but she went on to say that it is not as significant as it is in pure organizational change projects. The managing director of the project management consultancy previously mentioned also said they were involved post-completion often as expert witnesses in litigation, but people were selected for that based on their project management knowledge.

Strategic importance

All interviewees recognized strategic importance as a way of classifying projects. Each had different ways of classifying strategic importance. None mentioned it as a criterion for selecting project managers per se, but often projects of higher strategic importance were considered more complex, which was then the criterion for choosing the project manager.

Culture

All the companies undertook projects in their home country. Some hosted clients or resources from outside their country, some conducted projects in external territories. Seldom was the leadership style of the project manager significant when choosing managers for projects involving other cultures. Some firms worked regularly with other cultures and so their project managers were expected to be culturally sensitive, that was an entry ticket to joining the pool of potential project managers. Competencies that were considered were knowledge of the local language and local legal system. As previously mentioned, two interviewees considered leadership skills when choosing managers for certain geographies, but not others. Project managers for those geographies must be self-confident, stable, and tolerant.

Contract type

We did not initially include contract type in our research model, but five interviewees separately mentioned it as being significant, with different contract types requiring different leadership styles. Managers of fixed-price contracts must be task-focused and determined to have their way. Managers of remeasurement and alliance contracts must be flexible, willing to listen to other people's ideas and accept their views. Project managers of remeasurement and alliance contracts must be tolerant of others views.

Other attributes

Some interviewees suggested other attributes not included in Table 3-3 were important for choosing the project manager's leadership style and competence. For instance, the nature of the client and project scope and timing were mentioned.

Success criteria

We asked the interviewees how they judged project success to ensure that our model is relevant. It is not necessary that we cover all criteria for success, but the ones we do include should be significant. Table E-4 in Appendix E shows the success criteria as mentioned by each interviewee. Table 5-3 summarizes the success criteria mentioned, and the number of times each was mentioned. The last two might appear to be success factors, but they can influence the appreciation of the project team.

The criteria mentioned in Table 5-3 include the five we originally chose to focus on, as shown in Figure 3-2. The first two relate directly to appreciation by the sponsor. We chose to ignore stakeholder satisfaction. The others will all influence appreciation by the client, users, and project team. Appreciation by suppliers does not seem to be significant, although objectives, cost, time, safety, dealing with issues, and project prioritization may influence their appreciation of the project. However, it includes other significant measures of project success. We therefore decided that our original model of success criteria was not sufficiently comprehensive, and decided to extend it to the ten criteria shown in Table 4-2.

Criteria for selecting project managers

We asked the interviewees their criteria for selecting project managers. The responses by interviewee are shown in Table E-5 in Appendix E. Table 5-4 summarizes the criteria mentioned and the number of times each was mentioned. The first four, those mentioned most often, specifically relate to leadership skills. Cultural sensitivity is a leadership skill, but as we mentioned, the ability to work in other geographies is sometimes a technical skill. The next three mix technical project management and leadership skills. The last two relate to self-management and emotional intelligence.

1. Most firms said the competence of the project manager is important, and mentioned technical expertise, project management expertise and experience. This is consistent with the competence models of Crawford (2005). Interviewees said different competence profiles were important for different types of project. Different projects required different technical skills, more or less advanced project management skills and different amounts of experience. The mention of experience confirms the work of Lee-Kelly, Leong, and Loong (2003) that experience can influence a manager's self-confidence and perception of success.
2. Most firms said leadership style is important on complex projects but not on simple projects, although they had different ways of defining complexity. This suggests that if Keegan and Den Hartog (2004) had limited themselves to complex projects they might have achieved a positive result, but confirms their null result for all projects.

Criteria for selection	Times
Ability to deal or communicate with stakeholders, political sensitivity	8 times

Contract type
    fixed price
    remeasurement or alliance—sensitive, trustworthy, calm
	4 times

Able to deal with client	4 times
Able to deal with complexity, ambiguity and expected issues, duration	7 times
Cultural sensitivity, geography, language	4 times
Location and nature of work within the company	2 times

Type of assignment
    consultancy versus project management
    technical versus change project
	2 times

Duration and budget, project size	3 times
Able to balance work and home life	2 times
Development opportunity for the project manager	1 time

Table 5-4   Criteria for selecting project managers and number of times mentioned

3. Many firms said competence and leadership style is important for project managers, but all project managers in the pool of potential have a minimum level of the necessary competencies, so they are not considered when choosing a project manager for a given project. For instance a Dutch consultancy said all project managers must be politically sensitive. They do two types of work, consultancy and the provision of project management personnel. Those two types of assignment require different leadership and competence profiles, but there are two pools of potential project managers to draw on. A French mechanical design and construction contractor said that because the firm was family owned, maintaining a good relationship with the client was more important than maximizing profit on each job. This is because the firm wants to exist in perpetuity (*perenité*) and not increase dividends to shareholders year after year. For this reason the firm would train their own project managers, recruiting potential project managers directly from university, and only one in five recruits would eventually become project manager with the necessary client management skills. Thus, in many organizations, competence and leadership style is an entry ticket to the pool of potential project managers, not criteria for selecting the manager for a given project.

Task versus people orientation

We also asked the interviewees whether their project managers were task- or people-oriented (Fiedler 1967, see Chapter 2), and whether that affected the choice of project manager. Answers given are shown in Table E-6 in Appendix E. The following summarizes:
- task orientation was said to be more important twice
- people orientation said to be more important five times
- a balance said to be important seven times, although
  ○ once a preference was given to people orientation
  ○ once technical competence was said to be taken as given, but then a balance is important.

There is some variability by nation. Both French companies say people orientation is important. The German company (a subsidiary of an American company) says task orientation is important, but the U.K.-based subsidiary of the same company says project managers need a balance. The American subsidiary of the same company says people orientation is more important. Swedish companies are more likely to look for a balance. These results show more of balance than suggested by Mäkilouko (2004, see Chapter 3).

One interviewee mentioned a fundamental transformation:
- As project team members, people are people-oriented and complain that their project managers are too task-oriented.
- But upon becoming project managers those same people become task-oriented and adopt the behaviors they complained about as team members.

We might speculate why this is:
- the nature of the role of project manager requires people to be task-oriented
- task orientation of project managers is the only role model people have
- people orientation is the line manager's role but task orientation is the project manager's role (as suggested by another interviewee).

In choosing project managers firms said the following:
- They use task-focused project managers on IT projects but people-focused project managers on organizational change projects.
- They use task-focused project managers on simple projects, but people-focused project managers on complex projects.
- They use task-focused project managers on fixed-price contracts but people-focused project managers on remeasurement contracts and alliances.

Rating leadership competencies

We asked the interviewees to rate the leadership competencies in Table 4-1 in importance, as high, medium, and low. We then assigned 3 for high, 2 for medium, and 1 for low, and calculated the average for each competence and the average for each group. The detail results are shown in Table E-7 in Appendix E, and the summary for each competency in Table 5-4.

The results are not statistically significant, but seem to suggest that emotional and managerial competencies are more important for project managers than intellectual competencies. Project managers must be able to handle their emotions and manage people and the project, but do not need to be particularly intelligent.

Leadership competency	Rating	Average group	Average competency
Emotional competencies		2.4	
1. Self-awareness	M		2.4
2. Emotional resilience	M		2.4
3. Motivation	H		2.7
4. Sensitivity	M		2.4
5. Influence	M		2.4
6. Intuitiveness	L		2.0
7. Conscientiousness	M		2.5
Managerial competencies		2.4	
8. Engaging communication	M		2.5
9. Managing resources	H		2.6
10. Empowering	M		2.4
11. Developing	L		2.0
12. Achieving	H		2.7
Intellectual competencies		2.1	
13. Critical analysis and judgment	M		2.5
14. Vision and imagination	L		1.9
15. Strategic perspective	L		2.0

Table 5-5   Rating of the leadership competencies of project managers

We also rated the individual competencies. By the scale above, all would score medium to high, but to differentiate here we categorized scores of 1.9 to 2.2 as low, 2.3 to 2.5 as high, and 2.6 to 2.7 as high. Vision and imagination, strategic perspective, developing others and intuitiveness scored low. We were very surprised by the low score of developing others and saddened by the low score of vision and imagination and strategic perspective. Managing resources, achieving (self motivation) and motivation of others scored high. These were not surprising.

We also analyzed the interviews quantitatively for differences by industry, project type, and international versus domestic. The results should be interpreted as tendencies only, due to the small sample size.

1. Analysis for differences by industry (at a significance level of .10) indicates that the need for emotional resilience is significantly higher for projects in the engineering and construction industry than in the service industry (p < .075), and the need for an ability to influence is significantly higher in the information systems industry than in the service industry (p < .090). Both are EQ-related leadership dimensions.
2. Assessment for difference by project type indicates that leadership dimensions differ by the strategic importance of projects. The need for vision and imagination is significantly higher in renewal projects, than in repositioning projects (p < .091), and for sensitivity it is significantly higher in repositioning projects than in renewal projects (p < .031). These are IQ and EQ dimensions.
3. Further differences were found by the domestic or international scope of the projects. Strategic perspective and motivation were found to be significantly higher for international than for domestic projects (p < .010 and .043, respectively). These are also IQ and EQ dimensions. This indicates the need for different EQ and IQ profiles for different project types.

Summary

The interviews suggest that organizations do take account of the project manager's personality when selecting project managers to manage projects, choosing different leadership styles for different types of projects. Our model for success criteria covers most of the significant criteria used for judging project success. Other criteria are used, but if we can obtain a positive result based on these criteria, the hypothesis will be supported. However, a null result will not disprove the hypothesis. Similarly, our model for project attributes covers many of the attributes considered to be significant. Again, if we obtain a positive result using these attributes our hypothesis will be supported, but a null result will not disprove our hypothesis. The interviewees agreed that the fifteen leadership competencies were a useful way of assessing leadership competence.

Apart from the change to the number of success criteria, the interviews suggested that our research model is valid and therefore an appropriate basis for the Web-based questionnaire. The results of the questionnaire are described in the next chapter.

CHAPTER 6

Web-based Questionnaire

In this chapter we present the results of the Web-based questionnaire by identifying those EQ, MQ, and IQ competencies correlated with project performance in different project types. We then validate the results by mapping the quantitative results from the questionnaire analysis against the qualitative results from the interviews analysis. Through that we identify the important dimensions for project performance. Finally, we calculate profiles of project managers for high-performing projects for each project type across all fifteen leadership competencies. The profiles are described in the next chapter. The raw data from the Web-based questionnaire and the method of analysis is presented in Appendix G.

Competences and competencies correlated to high-performing projects

First, we look at which of the three competences and which of the fifteen competencies are correlated with high-performing projects. We look at each of the project types in Table 4-3. However, we had sufficient data points to be able to look at combinations of project types. Thus, we look at all projects and then the three application areas, engineering, IT, and organizational change projects. Then, when we come to the other attribute types, complexity, life-cycle stage, strategic importance, culture and contract type, we are able to look at all projects and each of the three application areas again.

However, a word of caution: All the results presented are statistically significant to the quoted level of significance. However, for the results to be strictly valid there should be five data points for each independent variable (Hair et al. 1998), so there should be fifteen projects in any project category for the analysis by the three competence types to be fully significant, and seventy-five for the analysis by fifteen competency dimensions. We have included the analysis for all categories with more than fifteen data points, but the analysis against the fifteen competency dimensions must be treated accordingly. Obviously if there are just under seventy-five data points we can be comfortable that the results are reasonably valid, but if the number of data points is just above fifteen the results must be treated with caution.

All projects and three application areas

Table 6-1 shows the results for all projects and for high-performing and low-performing projects. It also shows similar results for projects by the three application areas, engineering projects, information systems projects, and organizational and business projects. We see on high-performing projects from the complete sample, and on high-performing projects from each application area, emotional competencies are significant contributors to project success, but managerial and intellectual competencies are not. Looking at the fifteen individual competencies, we see that on all high-performing projects conscientiousness, sensitivity, and communication are correlated to project success, but strategic perspective is negatively correlated to project success. Thus, Hypothesis 1 is supported; certain competencies are more likely to be correlated to success than others.

We look now at high-performing projects in the other three application areas.
1. For engineering projects, conscientiousness and sensitivity are positively correlated with success, and vision is negatively correlated.
2. For information systems projects, self-awareness, communication, and developing are positively correlated, and vision is negatively correlated.

Competencies	Performance of all projects			Performance of engineering projects			Performance of information projects			Performance of organizational projects		
	All	Low	High	All	Low	High	All	Low	High	All	Low	High
Number of cases (n)	399	142	257	67	25	42	267	96	171	199	70	129
3-dimensional model												
• Emotional	++++	+	++++	+		++++	++++	+	++++	++++		++++
• Managerial												
• Intellectual												
Model: $R^2 =$	0.087	0.038	0.137	0.084	No	0.232	0.085	0.048	0.144	0.084	No	0.089
Adj. $R^2 =$	0.082	0.031	0.134	0.070	model	0.213	0.082	0.038	0.139	0.079	model	0.082
$p =$	0.000	0.020	0.000	0.017	found	0.000	0.000	0.033	0.000	0.000	found	0.001
15-dimensional model												
• Emotional												
• Motivation	++++	+	++++			++++	++++	+		++++		++++
• Conscientiousness			++++			++++						
• Sensitivity			++++	++		++++						
• Influence												
• Self-awareness									++++			
• Emotional resilience												
• Intuitiveness												
• Managerial												
• Managing resources	++++		++++						++++			++++
• Communication									++++			
• Developing												
• Empowering												
• Achieving							++++					
• Intellectual												
• Strategic perspective	====		====			====			====			====
• Vision												
• Critical thinking												
Model: $R^2 =$	0.093	0.034	0.168	0.104	No	0.430	0.107	0.061	0.206	0.095	No	0.171
Adj. $R^2 =$	0.089	0.027	0.155	0.090	model	0.385	0.101	0.051	0.187	0.091	model	0.151
$p =$	0.000	0.029	0.000	0.008	found	0.000	0.000	0.015	0.000	0.000	found	0.000

Key

Symbol	Meaning
++++	Positively correlated to performance, $p<0.001$
+++	Positively correlated to performance, $p<0.005$
++	Positively correlated to performance, $p<0.01$
+	Positively correlated to performance, $p<0.05$
====	Negatively correlated to performance, $p<0.001$
===	Negatively correlated to performance, $p<0.005$
==	Negatively correlated to performance, $p<0.01$
=	Negatively correlated to performance, $p<0.05$

Table 6-1   Results, all projects and the three types by application area

3. Organizational and business projects show a similar profile, but subtly different. Motivation and communication are positively correlated, but vision negatively correlated.

Thus, different competencies are appropriate for different types of projects. When you consider these results they seem sensible. Engineering projects require careful application of defined techniques. On the other hand, information and organizational change projects require good communication. We have asked information systems professionals why self-awareness is important on information systems projects. The response has been that computer professionals are unique. This is why IT projects need to be managed by IT professionals, because you have to understand what motivates the team, and to do that you need to be one of them, and have the self-awareness to understand yourself and your team. Organizational change projects require the manager to be able to motivate the stakeholders to accept the change.

The interesting result, which is likely to cause some controversy, is that vision is negatively correlated with success for all three application areas. Our take on this is that the project manager's role is to concentrate on delivering the project, and vision is a diversion that may lead the project manager in the wrong direction. Yes, the project needs to be linked to the organization's strategy. But that is the responsibility of other governance roles, particularly the project sponsor. The project manager needs to be aware of that, but needs to accept the vision as communicated to them by the project sponsor, not trying to develop his or her own vision. Similar arguments apply to strategic perspective on all projects.

Complexity

We repeated the analysis for complexity, looking at high, medium, and low complexity projects. We looked at high-performing projects only, looking first at all projects, and then engineering, IT, and organizational change projects, respectively (see Table 6-2). There were insufficient data points for any analysis on low complexity projects. It was no surprise that very few of our respondents thought their projects were of low complexity.

Looking first at the three competences, EQ, MQ, and IQ, we see again that emotional intelligence is important throughout. Again somewhat controversially intellectual competences are negatively correlated with success on medium complexity projects for all projects and IT projects.

Looking now at the fifteen competency dimensions:
1. On all medium complexity projects, emotional resilience and communication are important, but vision negatively correlated to success.
2. On high complexity projects, sensitivity is important, and suggested by several of our interviewees.
3. There were insufficient data points to draw valid conclusions about engineering projects, but again conscientiousness seems to be important.
4. On IT projects, again communication is important. On medium complexity projects, emotional resilience is also important and vision negatively correlated with success.
5. On organizational change projects, communication is also important. Emotional resilience is important on medium complexity projects and vision negatively correlated with success. Influence is important on high complexity projects, which is understandable. Empowering is negatively correlated with success, suggesting that high complexity organizational change projects the project manager needs to keep tight control.

Note that on high complexity projects, vision is neither positively nor negatively correlated with success. This suggests that on high complexity projects, the manager needs to have more strategic awareness.

Strategic importance

Next, we look at projects by strategic importance (see Table 6-3). Projects are categorized as mandatory, repositioning, and renewal projects. Again, we see that for repositioning and renewal projects, emotional competence is important throughout. But for mandatory projects, managerial competence is more important. Perhaps the nature of mandatory projects with a focus on survival and cost control requires careful management. Looking at the fifteen competency dimensions, there is little pattern between the three application areas. On repositioning projects, motivation is important. Repositioning projects are similar to organizational change projects and so this is consistent with the result above. On renewal projects, self-awareness and communication are important, making them similar to IT projects.

Contract type

The results by contract type are less conclusive (see Table 6-4). Often, especially on alliance projects, there is insufficient data. Very few of our respondents work on alliance projects. Also, sometimes no model

Competencies	Complexity (high-performing projects)			and engineering projects (high-performing projects)			and information projects (high-performing projects)			and organizational projects (high-performing projects)		
	Low	Med	High	Low	Med	High	Low	Med	High	Low	Med	High
Number of cases (n)	14	139	104	2	20	20	4	97	70	8	69	52
3-dimensional model												
• *Emotional*		++++	++++		+	+		++++	+++		++++	
• *Managerial*		====						====				
• *Intellectual*												
Model: $R^2 =$	Too few data	0.184	0.131	Too few data	0.293	0.265	Too few data	0.212	0.136	Too few data	0.189	No model found
Adj. $R^2 =$		0.172	0.123		0.254	0.224		0.195	0.124		0.177	
$p =$		0.000	0.000		0.014	0.020		0.000	0.002		0.000	
15-dimensional model												
• *Emotional*												
• *Motivation*												
• *Conscientiousness*			++++			++						++
• *Sensitivity*		++++			+							
• *Influence*												
• *Self-awareness*												
• *Emotional resilience*								++++			++++	
• *Intuitiveness*												
• *Managerial*												
• *Managing resources*												
• *Communication*		++++						++++	++++		++++	
• *Developing*												
• *Empowering*												
• *Achieving*												
• *Intellectual*												
• *Strategic perspective*		====						====			====	==
• *Vision*												
• *Critical thinking*												
Model: $R^2 =$	Too few data	0.195	0.123	Too few data	0.273	0.356	Too few data	0.223	0.141	Too few data	0.282	0.191
Adj. $R^2 =$		0.177	0.114		0.233	0.320		0.198	0.128		0.249	0.158
$p =$		0.000	0.000		0.018	0.006		0.000	0.001		0.000	0.006

Key

Symbol	Meaning
++++	Positively correlated to performance, $p<0.001$
+++	Positively correlated to performance, $p<0.005$
++	Positively correlated to performance, $p<0.01$
+	Positively correlated to performance, $p<0.05$
====	Negatively correlated to performance, $p<0.001$
===	Negatively correlated to performance, $p<0.005$
==	Negatively correlated to performance, $p<0.01$
=	Negatively correlated to performance, $p<0.05$

Table 6-2   Results, complexity, all projects and three application areas, high-performing projects

Competencies	Project importance (high-performing projects)			Engineering projects (high-performing projects)			Information projects (high-performing projects)			Organizational projects (high-performing projects)		
	Mandatory	Repositioning	Renewal	Mandatory	Repositioning	Renewal	Mandatory	Repositioning	Renewal	Mandatory	Repositioning	Renewal
Number of cases (n)	43	141	127	11	21	22	29	103	78	17	78	60
3-dimensional model												
• Emotional	+++	++++	++++		++	+++	++	++++	++++		++	+
• Managerial												
• Intellectual												
Model: $R^2 =$	0.203	0.155	0.178	Too few data	0.332	0.387	0.243	0.154	0.188	No model found	0.090	0.107
Adj. $R^2 =$	0.184	0.149	0.171		0.296	0.356	0.215	0.145	0.178		0.078	0.091
$p =$	0.002	0.000	0.000		0.006	0.002	0.007	0.000	0.000		0.007	0.011
15-dimensional model												
• Emotional												
• Motivation					++++			++++			++++	
• Conscientiousness		++++			++++				++++			
• Sensitivity												
• Influence			++++						++++			
• Self-awareness												
• Emotional resilience										==		
• Intuitiveness												
• Managerial												
• Managing resources												
• Communication	++++		++++				++++			++++	++++	++++
• Developing												
• Empowering												
• Achieving												
• Intellectual												
• Strategic perspective					====	+++					====	
• Vision												
• Critical thinking												
Model: $R^2 =$	0.299	0.171	0.230	Too few data	0.703	0.339	0.319	0.164	0.291	0.544	0.260	0.170
Adj. $R^2 =$	0.282	0.165	0.217		0.650	0.306	0.294	0.155	0.272	0.479	0.230	0.156
$p =$	0.000	0.000	0.000		0.000	0.004	0.001	0.000	0.000	0.004	0.000	0.001

Key

Symbol	Meaning
++++	Positively correlated to performance, $p<0.001$
+++	Positively correlated to performance, $p<0.005$
++	Positively correlated to performance, $p<0.01$
+	Positively correlated to performance, $p<0.05$
====	Negatively correlated to performance, $p<0.001$
===	Negatively correlated to performance, $p<0.005$
==	Negatively correlated to performance, $p<0.01$
=	Negatively correlated to performance, $p<0.05$

Table 6-3   Results, project importance, all projects and three application areas, high-performing projects

	Contract type (high-performing projects)			Engineering projects (high-performing projects)			Information projects (high-performing projects)			Organizational projects (high-performing projects)		
Competencies	Fixed Price	Remeasure-ment	Alliance	Fixed Price	Remeasure-ment	Alliance	Fixed Price	Remeasure-ment	Alliance	Fixed Price	Remeasure-ment	Alliance
Number of cases (n)	103	84	24	18	116	5	73	55	11	39	16	0
3-dimensional model												
• Emotional	++++	+++		+			++++			+++		
• Managerial		+++										
• Intellectual												
Model: $R^2 =$	0.219	0.144	No model found	0.330	No model found	Too few data	0.265	No model found	Too few data	0.181	No model found	Too few data
Adj. $R^2 =$	0.211	0.123		0.288			0.254			0.162		
$p =$	0.000	0.002		0.013			0.000			0.004		
15-dimensional model												
• Emotional												
• Motivation												
• Conscientiousness	++++	++++		++++	++++		++++					
• Sensitivity												
• Influence							++++					
• Self-awareness												
• Emotional resilience												
• Intuitiveness												
• Managerial												
• Managing resources	++++	+++								++++		
• Communication												
• Developing		===			===							
• Empowering					===						====	
• Achieving												
• Intellectual												
• Strategic perspective												
• Vision												
• Critical thinking												
Model: $R^2 =$	0.281	0.155	No model found	0.613	0.906	Too few data	0.324	No model found	Too few data	0.276	No model found	Too few data
Adj. $R^2 =$	0.267	0.123		0.589	0.883		0.305			0.259		
$p =$	0.000	0.004		0.000	0.000		0.000			0.000		

Key

Symbol	Meaning
++++	Positively correlated to performance, $p<0.001$
+++	Positively correlated to performance, $p<0.005$
++	Positively correlated to performance, $p<0.01$
+	Positively correlated to performance, $p<0.05$
====	Negatively correlated to performance, $p<0.001$
===	Negatively correlated to performance, $p<0.005$
==	Negatively correlated to performance, $p<0.01$
=	Negatively correlated to performance, $p<0.05$

Table 6-4   Results, contract type, all projects and three application areas, high-performing projects only

was found. We look only at all projects, though results are presented by the three application areas. On fixed-price contracts, managerial competencies are important, whereas on remeasurement contracts emotional and intellectual competencies are significant. This is consistent with what we were told in the interviews; on fixed-price contracts the manager must be focused on the result, whereas on remeasurement contracts he or she must be sensitive and tolerant. Looking at the fifteen competency dimensions, on fixed-price contracts, sensitivity and communication are important; while on remeasurement contracts, influence and communication are important. Empowering is negatively correlated on remeasurement contracts. Perhaps on such projects, the team cannot be given too much flexibility or control of cost will be lost.

Project stage

Results by project stage (Table 6-5 a&b) are very consistent with the results for all projects we started with. There is surprisingly little variation by project stage, inconsistent with what Frame (1987) and Turner (1999) suggested. We conclude that emotional competence is important throughout the project as are conscientiousness and communication. Managing resources also seems to be important in design, and motivation, sensitivity, and close-out. The latter is understandable; during closeout the project manager needs to motivate people to complete on time and cost at a time when mistakes have a big impact, and that requires sensitivity.

Culture

Results by culture (Table 6-6) are inconclusive, with insufficient data points for overseas projects, and home projects do not add anything to what we have already seen.

Summary

Tables 6-7 to 6-10, which are used later for validation, represent the data now for all projects, engineering projects, information systems projects, and organizational change projects, respectively. The final column in Tables 6-7 to 6-10 shows the number of times each dimension appears for each application area. This is not statistically significant, but gives an indication of differences by project type.

We see that almost always, emotional competence, EQ, significantly contributes to project success. Occasionally managerial competence, MQ, contributes significantly, and on a small number of occasions, intellectual competence, IQ, is negatively correlated. This is consistent with our interviews. Looking at the fifteen constituent competencies, on engineering projects, conscientiousness repeatedly appears as being positively correlated with project success. Other competencies appear occasionally, vision being negatively correlated twice. On information systems projects, self-awareness and communication are repeatedly correlated with project success, and vision repeatedly negatively correlated. On organizational change projects, communication is repeatedly positively correlated and vision repeatedly negatively correlated. In Table 6-7, communication appears the most often. Motivation, conscientiousness, sensitivity, and managing resources also appear several times, and strategic perspective is often negatively correlated to project success. We do not have space here to list all the differences by different types of projects. Thus, we conclude that Hypothesis 2 is supported, different leadership competencies are appropriate on different types of projects.

We can understand why conscientiousness is important on engineering projects but less so on information and organizational projects, and why communication is important on the latter two types, but less so on engineering projects. On information systems and organizational projects, it is important to keep the stakeholders committed to the project, and inform them of the nature of the desired results and work of the project, which will often be abstract in nature. On engineering projects, the project deliverables are more concrete, and clearly delineated in the project's designs. Thoroughness is more important. Many people may be concerned by the conclusion that project managers should lack vision, especially on organizational and business projects. However, our conclusion is that it is the responsibility of other project roles, such as the sponsor, to link the project's outputs and outcomes to organizational strategy, while the project manager must remain focused on delivering the projects results.

Validation

For the development of a final model we compared the results of the quantitative study (questionnaire based), with the results of the qualitative study (interview based) in order to identify overlapping results. (The method is described more fully in Appendix G.) Similar results from both studies were considered to be validated results. Validation was done through a reconciliation of the "manager's view," which was captured through the interviews, and the reality applied in projects, which was captured through the Web-based, global questionnaire.

Competencies	Project phase (high-performing projects)					and engineering projects (high-performing projects)				
	Feas	Design	Exec	Close	Comm	Feas	Design	Exec	Close	Comm
Number of cases (n)	146	221	249	225	123	18	33	40	36	24
3-dimensional model • Emotional • Managerial • Intellectual	++++	++++	++++	++++	++++	+	+++	++++	+	+
Model: $R^2 =$ Adj. $R^2 =$ $p =$	0.160 0.154 0.000	0.147 0.143 0.000	0.131 0.128 0.000	0.121 0.118 0.000	0.151 0.144 0.000	0.321 0.279 0.014	0.257 0.233 0.003	0.256 0.237 0.001	0.167 0.143 0.013	0.260 0.226 0.011

15-dimensional model
• Emotional
  • Motivation
  • Conscientiousness
  • Sensitivity
  • Influence
  • Self-awareness
  • Emotional resilience
  • Intuitiveness
• Managerial
  • Managing resources
  • Communication
  • Developing
  • Empowering
  • Achieving
• Intellectual
  • Strategic perspective
  • Vision
  • Critical thinking
	++++	++++
		
		++++
		++++
		
		====
		
			++++
			
			++++
			
			++++
			
			====
				++++
				
				++++
				
				++++
				
					++++
					
					++++
					++++
					++++
					
					====
						
						+
							++++	++++	++++	++++

Model: $R^2 =$ Adj. $R^2 =$ $p =$	0.162 0.156 0.000	0.180 0.164 0.000	0.155 0.145 0.000	0.133 0.126 0.000	0.229 0.203 0.000	0.245 0.198 0.037	0.312 0.290 0.001	0.325 0.307 0.000	0.290 0.269 0.001	0.332 0.301 0.003

Key

Symbol	Meaning
++++	Positively correlated to performance, $p < 0.001$
+++	Positively correlated to performance, $p < 0.005$
++	Positively correlated to performance, $p < 0.01$
+	Positively correlated to performance, $p < 0.05$
====	Negatively correlated to performance, $p < 0.001$
===	Negatively correlated to performance, $p < 0.005$
==	Negatively correlated to performance, $p < 0.01$
=	Negatively correlated to performance, $p < 0.05$

Table 6-5a Results, project phase, all projects and engineering projects, high-performing only

Competencies	And information projects (high-performing projects)					and organizational projects (high-performing projects)				
	Feas	Design	Exec	Close	Comm	Feas	Design	Exec	Close	Comm
Number of cases (n)	101	152	167	157	77	81	109	124	112	65
3-dimensional model										
• Emotional	++++	++++	++++	++++	++++	+++	+++	+++	+	+
• Managerial										
• Intellectual										
Model: $R^2 =$	0.243	0.168	0.129	0.133	0.261	0.100	0.085	0.067	0.057	0.085
Adj. $R^2 =$	0.235	0.163	0.123	0.128	0.241	0.088	0.077	0.059	0.048	0.070
$p =$	0.000	0.000	0.000	0.000	0.000	0.004	0.002	0.004	0.011	0.019
15-dimensional model										
• Emotional										
• Motivation		++++								
• Conscientiousness							+++			
• Sensitivity										
• Influence	++++	++++	++++	++++	++++					++
• Self-awareness										
• Emotional resilience	++++	++++	++++	++++						
• Intuitiveness										
• Managerial										
• Managing resources										
• Communication	++++	++++	++++	++++		++++	++++	++++	++++	
• Developing										
• Empowering										
• Achieving										
• Intellectual										
• Strategic perspective	====	====	====		====	====	====		====	
• Vision										
• Critical thinking										
Model: $R^2 =$	0.328	0.224	0.171	0.154	0.312	0.189	0.175	0.087	0.116	0.102
Adj. $R^2 =$	0.300	0.203	0.156	0.143	0.284	0.168	0.152	0.080	0.100	0.088
$p =$	0.000	0.000	0.000	0.000	0.000	0.000	0.000	0.001	0.001	0.009

Key

Symbol	Meaning
++++	Positively correlated to performance, $p<0.001$
+++	Positively correlated to performance, $p<0.005$
++	Positively correlated to performance, $p<0.01$
+	Positively correlated to performance, $p<0.05$
====	Negatively correlated to performance, $p<0.001$
===	Negatively correlated to performance, $p<0.005$
==	Negatively correlated to performance, $p<0.01$
=	Negatively correlated to performance, $p<0.05$

Table 6-5b Results, project phase, IT projects and organizational projects, high-performing projects only

Competencies	Culture (high-performing) Home	Culture (high-performing) Overseas	and engineering (high-performing) Home	and engineering (high-performing) Overseas	And information (high-performing) Home	And information (high-performing) Overseas	and organization (high-performing) Home	and organization (high-performing) Overseas
Number of cases (n)	233	24	34	8	161	10	119	10
3-dimensional model								
• Emotional	++++	+	+	Limited data	++++	Limited data	+++	Limited data
• Managerial								
• Intellectual								
Model: $R^2 =$	0.122	0.244	0.121		0.159		0.082	
Adj. $R^2 =$	0.118	0.209	0.094		0.154		0.074	
$p =$	0.000	0.014	0.044		0.000		0.002	
15-dimensional model								
• Emotional								
• Motivation	++++		++++		++++		++++	
• Conscientiousness	++++							
• Sensitivity								
• Influence					++++		++++	
• Self-awareness								
• Emotional resilience								
• Intuitiveness	++++	++						
• Managerial								
• Managing resources	++++				++++		++++	
• Communication								
• Developing								
• Empowering								
• Achieving								
• Intellectual								
• Strategic perspective	====						====	
• Vision								
• Critical thinking								
Model: $R^2 =$	0.180	0.274	0.276	Too few data	0.174	Too few data	0.163	Too few data
Adj. $R^2 =$	0.162	0.241	0.253		0.164		0.142	
$p =$	0.000	0.020	0.000		0.000		0.000	

Key

Symbol	Meaning
++++	Positively correlated to performance, $p<0.001$
+++	Positively correlated to performance, $p<0.005$
++	Positively correlated to performance, $p<0.01$
+	Positively correlated to performance, $p<0.05$
====	Negatively correlated to performance, $p<0.001$
===	Negatively correlated to performance, $p<0.005$
==	Negatively correlated to performance, $p<0.01$
=	Negatively correlated to performance, $p<0.05$

Table 6-6 Results, culture, all projects and three application areas, high-performing projects only

Competency	Typ	Complexity			Importance				Contract			Phase				Culture			Cnt
	All	Lo	Me	Hi	Ma	Rp	Rn	FP	Rm	Alli	F	D	Ex	CO	Cm	Hm	ExP	
Number of data points	257	14	139	104	43	141	127	103	84	24	146	221	229	225	123	223	24	
3 Competences		<15								NM								
• Emotional, EQ	P		P	P		P	P		P		P	P	P	P	P	P	P	13
• Managerial, MQ	P				P			P										2
• Intellectual, IQ			N						P									1, 1
15 Competencies		<15			<75					NM							<75	
Emotional																		
• Motivation						P						P	P	P	P	P		3
• Conscientiousness	P			P				P					P		P			5
• Sensitivity	P														P			4
• Influence							P		P									1
• Self-awareness			P															1
• Emotional resilience																		1
• Intuitiveness																		0
Managerial																		
• Managing resources	P		P		P		P	P	P		P	P	P	P	P	P	P	3
• Communication								P				P			P			9
• Developing									N									1
• Empowering																		1
• Achieving																		0
Intellectual																		
• Strategic perspective	N											N	N		N	N		5
• Vision			N															1
• Critical thinking																		0

Key P = Positively correlated with success on high-performing projects
     N = Negatively correlated with success on high-performing projects
     NM = No model found
     <15 = Fewer than 15 data points, no model calculated
     <75 = Fewer than 75 data points, model for 15 competencies may not be significant
     bold = **Validated results**

Table 6-7   Results and validation, all projects, high-perfomance projects only

Competency	Typ	Complexity			Importance			Contract			Phase					Culture		Cnt
	Eng	Lo	Me	Hi	Ma	Rp	Rn	FP	Rm	Alli	F	D	Ex	CO	Cm	Hm	ExP	
Number of data points	42	2	20	20	11	21	22	18	116	5	18	33	40	36	24	34	8	
3 Competences																		
• Emotional, EQ	P	<15	P	P	<15	P	P	P	NM	<15	P	P	P	P	P	P	<15	11
• Managerial, MQ																		1
• Intellectual, IQ																		0
15 Competencies		<15	<75	<75	<15	<75	<75	<75		<15	<75	<75	<75	<75	<75	<75	<15	
Emotional																		
• **Motivation**	P		P	P		P	P	P	P			P	P	P	P	P		3
• Conscientiousness	P					P		P										8
• Sensitivity																		2
• Influence																		0
• Self-awareness																		0
• Emotional resilience																		0
• Intuitiveness																		0
Managerial																		
• Managing resources											P							1
• Communication									N									0
• Developing																		0
• Empowering						N												1
• Achieving																		0
Intellectual																		
• Strategic perspective	N																	0
• **Vision**							P		N									3
• Critical thinking																		1

Key P   = Positively correlated with success on high-performing projects
    N   = Negatively correlated with success on high-performing projects
    NM   = No model found
    <15 = Fewer than 15 data points, no model calculated
    <75 = Fewer than 75 data points, model for 15 competencies may not be significant
    bold = **Validated results**

Table 6-8   Results and validation, engineering projects, high-performance projects only

Competency	Typ	Complexity			Importance				Contract			Phase				Culture		Cnt
	IT	Lo	Me	Hi	Ma	Rp	Rn	FP	Rm	Alli	F	D	Ex	CO	Cm	Hm	ExP	
Number of data points	171	4	97	70	29	103	78	73	55	11	101	152	167	157	77	161	10	
3 Competences		<15								<15								
• Emotional, EQ	P		P	P	P	P	P	P	NM		P	P	P	P	P	P	<15	13
• Managerial, MQ			N															0
• Intellectual, IQ															P			1, 1
15 Competencies		<15		<75	<75			<75	NM	<15							<15	
Emotional																		
• Motivation												P						2
• Conscientiousness																		0
• Sensitivity							P	P							P			3
• Influence				P											P			2
• Self-awareness	P						P					P	P	P		P		7
• Emotional resilience			P								P							1
• Intuitiveness											P							1
Managerial																		
• Managing resources																		0
• Communication	P		P								P	P	P	P		P		8
• Developing	P																	1
• Empowering																		0
• Achieving																		0
Intellectual																		
• Strategic perspective	N																	1
• Vision			N								N	N			N			4
• Critical thinking																		0

Key P = Positively correlated with success on high-performing projects
    N = Negatively correlated with success on high-performing projects
    NM = No model found
    <15 = Fewer than 15 data points, no model calculated
    <75 = Fewer than 75 data points, model for 15 competencies may not be significant
    bold = **Validated results**

Table 6-9   Results and validation, engineering projects, high-performance projects only

Competency	Typ	Complexity			Importance				Contract			Phase				Culture		Cnt
	Org	Lo	Me	Hi	Ma	Rp	Rn	FP	Rm	Alli	F	D	Ex	CO	Cm	Hm	ExP	
Number of data points	129	8	69	52	17	78	60	39	16	0	89	101	124	112	65	119	10	
3 Competences																		
• Emotional, EQ	P	<15	P	NM	NM	P	P	P	NM	<15	P	P	P	P	P	P	<15	11
• Managerial, MQ																		0
• Intellectual, IQ																		1
15 Competencies		<15	<75	<75	<75		<75	<75	NM	<15					<75		<15	
Emotional																		
• **Motivation**	P					P						P				P		3
• Conscientiousness																		1
• Sensitivity				P														0
• Influence															P	P		3
• Self-awareness			P															0
• Emotional resilience																		1
• Intuitiveness																		0
Managerial																		
• Managing resources																		0
• **Communication**	P		P	N		P	P	P			P	P	P	P		P		10
• Developing																		0
• Empowering														P				1
• Achieving																		0
Intellectual																		
• Strategic perspective																		0
• **Vision**	N		N			N					N	N		N	N			7
• Critical thinking																		0

Key
P = Positively correlated with success on high-performing projects
N = Negatively correlated with success on high-performing projects
NM = No model found
<15 = Fewer than 15 data points, no model calculated
<75 = Fewer than 75 data points, model for 15 competencies may not be significant
bold = **Validated results**

Table 6-10   Results and validation, organizational change projects, high-performance projects only

Validation was done at the levels of project type, project phase, complexity, importance, contract, and culture. For that the rankings from the interviews were grouped by project type (engineering and construction, information technology, and organizational change) and the average ranking of the fifteen competency dimension calculated for each project type. That gave the particular rankings of the importance of each of the fifteen competency dimensions (by the interviewees) for all projects and for each project type. These rankings were subsequently compared with the results from the quantitative analysis. A match of interviewer rating being medium or high from the qualitative study, with a dimension that was found to be statistically significantly related with project performance (through the quantitative study), was then considered a validated result, because of its appearance within both studies. Those dimensions that were found negatively related with project results in the quantitative study were checked for being ranked "low" in the qualitative study. Such a match was also considered to be a validated result. The outcome of the validation is shown Tables 6-7 to 6-10. Validated results are indicated in bold.

The validation shows clearly the importance of emotional competence for all project types. The higher the emotional competence was—the better the project results were. Looking at Table 6-7, which shows in bold those validated competences that are correlated with project performance, we see that a large number of the fifteen competencies are correlated with performance. This, however, is on the aggregate level, for all projects. Looking at Tables 6-8 to 6-10, we see that different dimensions are important in different project types. With the exception of strategic perspective, the results support Hypothesis 1: the project manager's competency is positively correlated to project success.

Strategic perspective is negatively correlated with project success, which is an unexpected result that can possibly be explained by the project manager's task of planning and implementing in accordance with a predefined project objective. Strategic roles may better be left to other governance roles, particularly the project sponsor.

Hypothesis 2 is also supported: different competence profiles are appropriate for different types of project.

Across all projects, EQ and MQ are important for performance, especially motivation, conscientiousness, sensitivity, influence, self-awareness, emotional resilience, as well as managing resources, and communication. Strategic thinking must not be exercised by the project manager. The role of IQ is inconclusive. It shows that project managers with changing project types need to be extremely well developed in almost all emotional competencies and some managerial competencies.

For engineering and construction projects, the sample size was too small to reliably identify the correlations at the level of the fifteen dimensions. At the level of the three summary dimensions, it shows that EQ is correlated with project performance, and to a lesser extent, MQ as well. Vision might not be exercised to a large extent in these projects, as it can have adverse effects on project performance.

In IT projects, performance correlates with the EQ of the project manager. IQ is positive at the commissioning stage of projects, but negatively correlated with performance in projects of medium complexity. The role of IQ is therefore not clear across IT projects. EQ and MQ dimensions that are correlated with performance are motivation, sensitivity, influence, self-awareness, emotional resilience, as well as communication. Vision, however, should not be exercised to a large extent by the project manager, because of its negative relation to project performance.

Performance in organizational change projects is, once again, correlated with the EQ competencies of the project manager. Especially, motivation and communication are positively correlated and vision negatively correlated with performance of the project.

Table 6-11 summarizes the dimensions important for project performance in engineering and construction, IT, and organizational change projects. IT projects appear to have a wide variety of dimensions related with success. That may indicate the need to further break down IT projects into different project types in order to identify particular dimensions for different types of IT projects.

Within this chapter we have identified the EQ, MQ, and IQ dimensions important for project success. In the next chapter we analyze the extent those important dimensions are developed in project managers of high-performing projects.

We have identified which of the three leadership competences, EQ, MQ, and IQ, and which of the fifteen constituent leadership competencies, are correlated with performance on high-performing projects on each of the nineteen project types in Table 4-3, and some additional combinations of those. However, we also consider whether it is possible to calculate full profiles against the fifteen competency dimensions for successful project managers for all nineteen project types in the same way Dulewicz and Higgs (2003) did for the three levels of change in organizations. We present those results in the next chapter.

All project types	Engineering	IT	Organizational Change
EQ MQ	EQ MQ	EQ	EQ
EQ • Motivation • Conscientiousness • Sensitivity • Influence • Self-awareness • Emotional resilience		EQ • Motivation • Sensitivity • Influence • Self-awareness • Emotional resilience	EQ • Motivation
MQ • Managing resources • Communication		MQ • Communication	MQ • Communication
IQ • - Strategic perspective	IQ • - Vision	IQ • - Vision	IQ • - Vision

Table 6-11   Summary of important dimensions across three application areas

CHAPTER 7

Project Manager Profiles

In this chapter we present the profiles of project managers in different types of high-performing projects. It complements the prior chapter, where we identified those EQ, MQ, and IQ dimensions important for project performance, by showing to what extent these dimensions are present in the managers of these projects. The method of analysis by which we determined the profiles is described in Appendix G.

Profiles by application area

Figures 7-1 to 7-3 show the profile of project managers in high-performing engineering, IT, and organizational change projects.

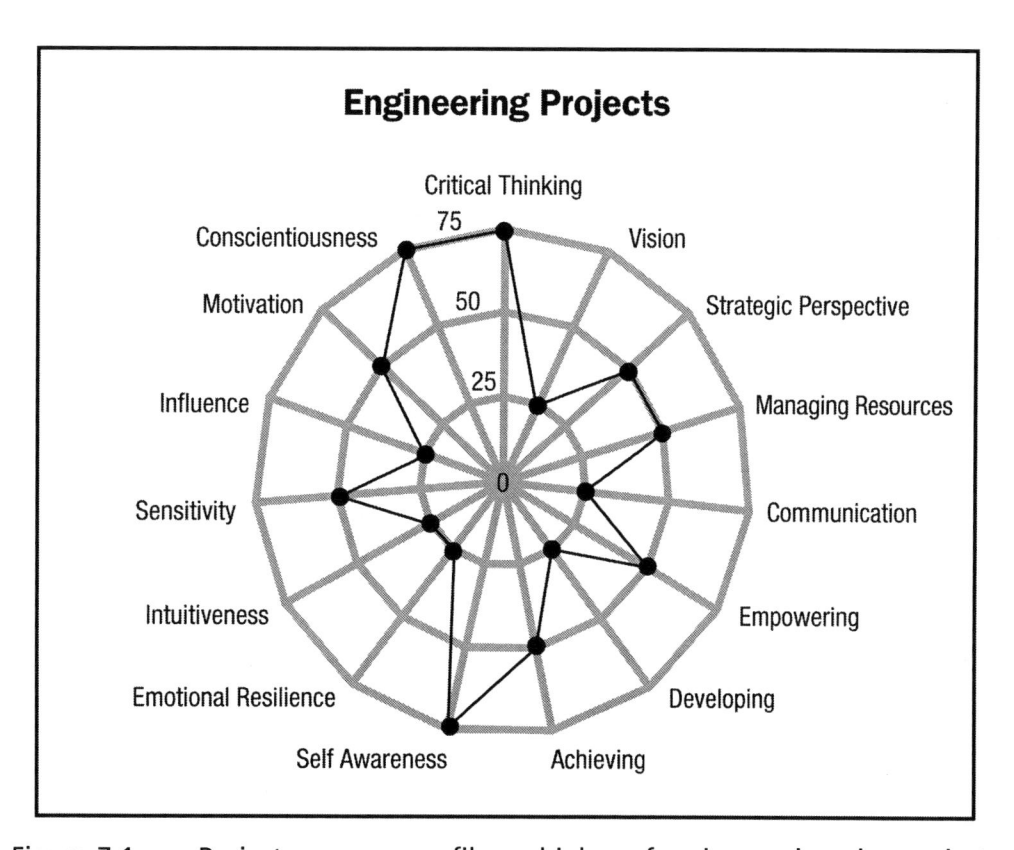

Figure 7-1   Project manager profile on high-performing engineering projects

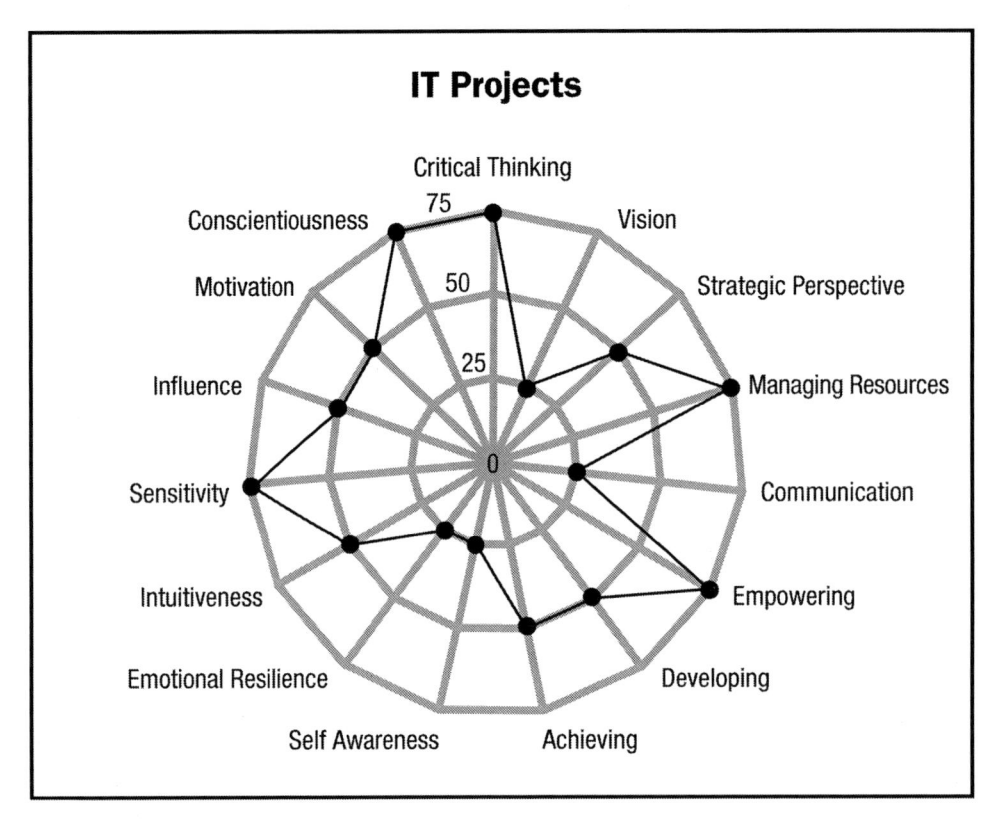

Figure 7-2   Project manager profile on high-performing IT projects

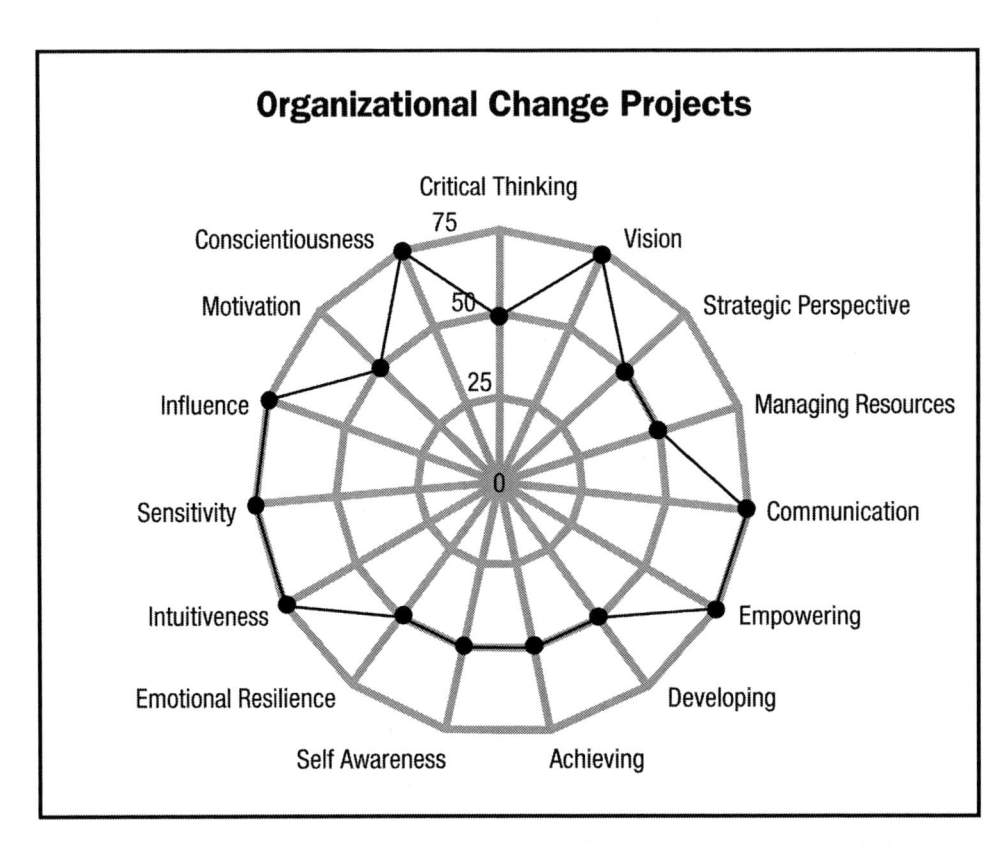

Figure 7-3   Project manager profile on high-performing organizational change projects

Engineering projects

Engineering project managers show strong competencies in critical thinking (IQ), self-awareness (EQ), and conscientiousness (EQ). At medium levels are the human resource management related dimensions, and at the lowest level the more strategic dimensions. Dimensions especially important for project performance could not be detected due to the small sample size for these projects. However, on a summary level higher EQ and MQ are correlated with higher performance in projects.

IT Projects

IT project managers show the highest levels of critical thinking (IQ) and conscientiousness (EQ). However, they also show a different management attitude as indicated by the highest levels in managing resources (MQ), empowering (MQ), and sensitivity (EQ). Similar to engineering project managers, vision (IQ), communication (MQ), and emotional resilience (EQ) are less strongly developed. However, in contrast to engineering project managers, they show low levels of self awareness (EQ). The medium strong levels are a mix of strategic and human resource management related competencies. The profile shows the different requirements stemming from nature of an IT project being both a technical as well as an organizational change project. To that end the profile lies in the middle between those of engineering project managers and organizational change project managers. Dimensions important for project performance are the EQ competencies for motivation, sensitivity, influence, self-awareness, emotional resilience, as well as the MQ competency communication. Vision (IQ) is negatively related to project performance. Some of these are not strongly present in IT project managers (e.g., self awareness, emotional resilience and communication). Developing these dimensions will contribute directly to project success.

Organizational change projects

Organizational change project managers show medium to strong competencies in all dimensions. Due to the intangible nature of their project's outcome they are very strong in vision (IQ), communication (MQ), empowering (MQ), intuitiveness (EQ), sensitivity (EQ), influence (EQ), and conscientiousness (EQ). Other competencies are medium strong. Compared with more technical projects, such as engineering and IT, managers in organizational change projects build vision, objectives and influence their environment to change toward the project goal. Directly related with project performance are motivation and communication. Developing these project managers from a medium level in motivation to a high level will bring about the biggest chance to improve project performance.

Profiles by project complexity

Figures 7-4 to 7-6 show the profiles for low, medium, and high complexity projects, respectively.

Low complexity

Project managers of high-performing, low-complexity projects show strong competencies in managing resources (MQ), communication (MQ), conscientiousness (EQ), and critical thinking (IQ). Achieving (MQ) and influence (EQ) are medium strong; all other competencies are not very strong in these projects. No particular dimension could be identified to be important for performance in these projects.

Medium complexity

To manage projects of medium complexity successfully, project managers show strong competencies in critical thinking (IQ), conscientiousness (EQ), and sensitivity (EQ). Other dimensions are low to medium. Dimensions especially related to project performance are emotional resilience (EQ) and communication (MQ). Both are low in their expression. Building stronger capabilities in these two areas will improve project performance.

High complexity

High-performing, high-complexity projects are managed by project managers scoring high in all dimensions. The questionnaire and interviews showed that sensitivity is more important for project performance than the other dimensions.

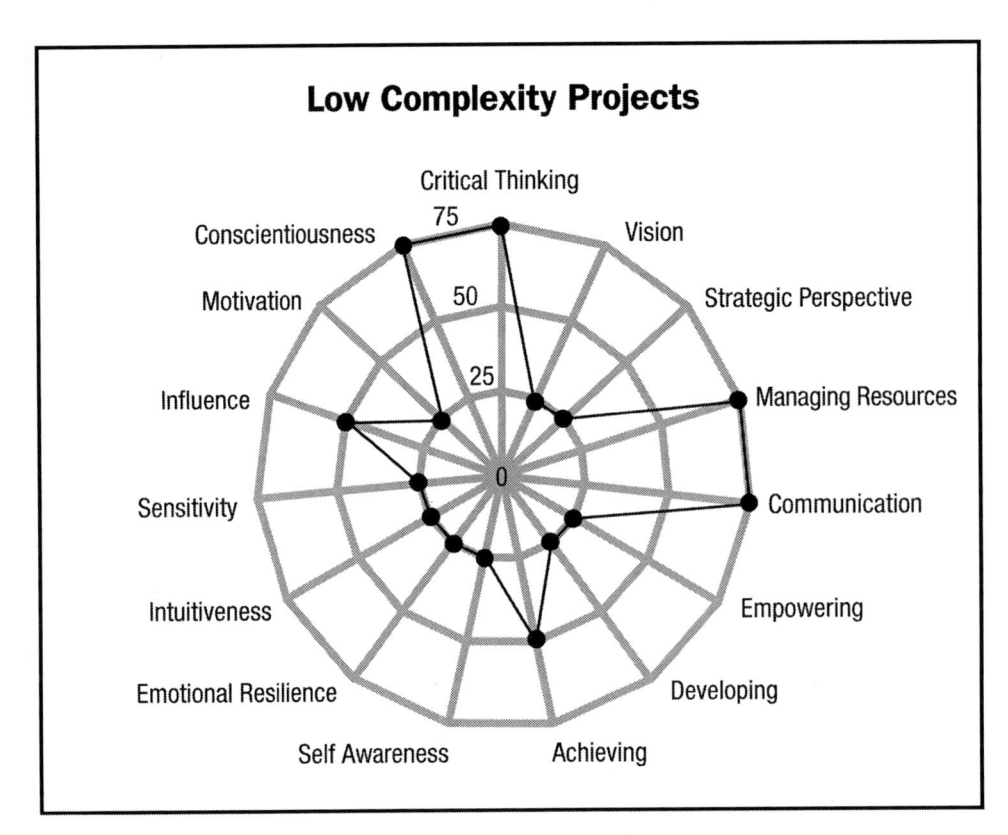

Figure 7-4   Project manager profile on high-performing, low complexity projects

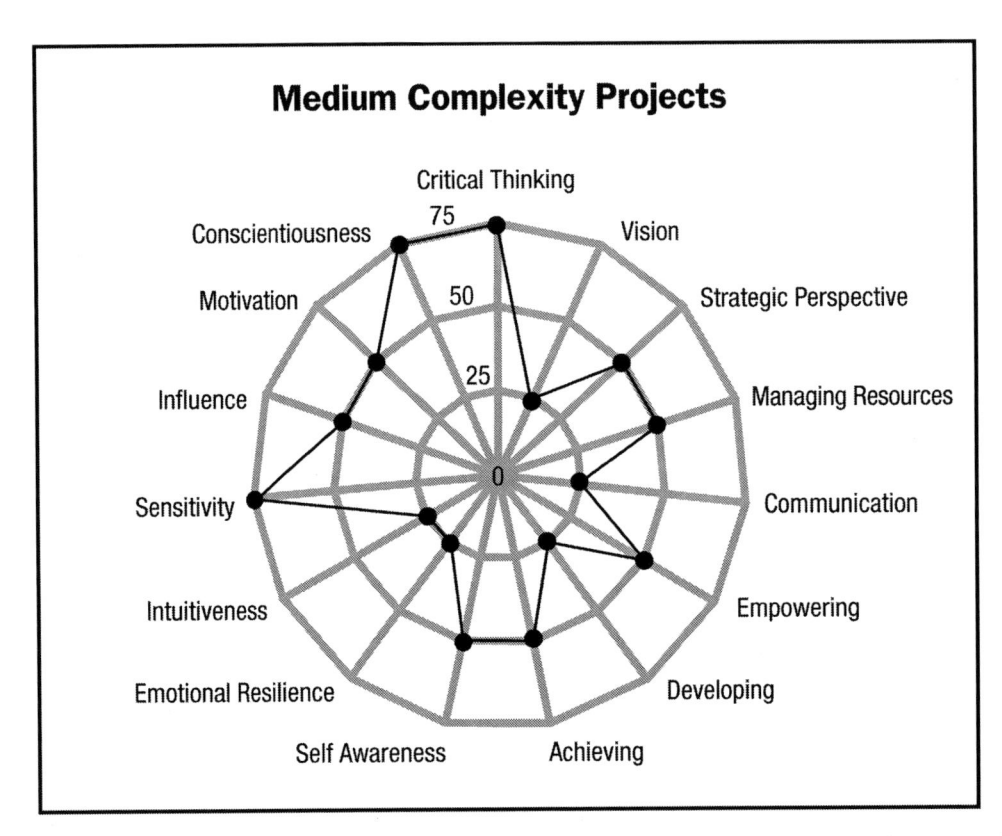

Figure 7-5   Project manager profile on high-performing, medium complexity projects

High Complexity Projects

[Radar chart showing competency dimensions: Critical Thinking, Vision, Strategic Perspective, Managing Resources, Communication, Empowering, Developing, Achieving, Self Awareness, Emotional Resilience, Intuitiveness, Sensitivity, Influence, Motivation, Conscientiousness. Scale: 0, 25, 50, 75.]

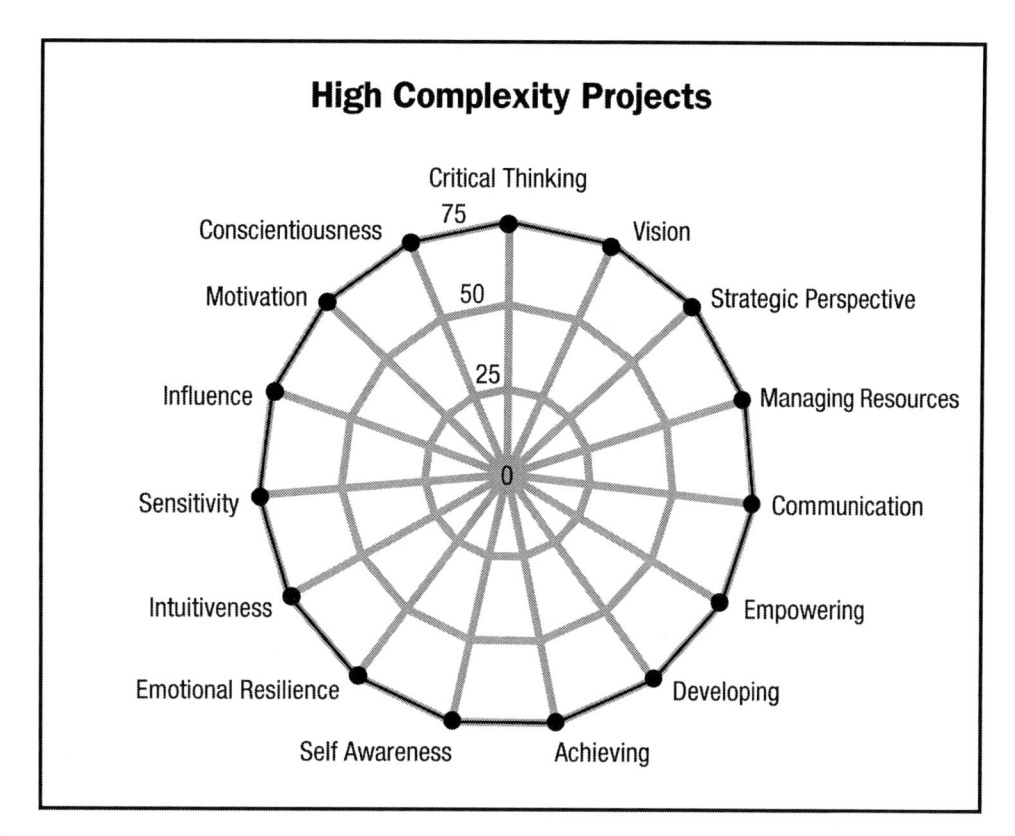

Figure 7-6   Project manager profile on high-performing, high complexity projects

Comparison

Complexity therefore appears to be the most distinguishing factor when it comes to different competencies for different project types. With increasing complexity the required competencies move from managerial in low complexity projects, to emotional in medium complexity, to all in high complexity projects.

Profiles by project importance

Figures 7-7 to 7-9 show the profiles of project managers in mandatory projects, renewal projects, and repositioning projects, respectively.

Mandatory projects

Project managers in high-performing, mandatory projects show strong competencies in critical thinking (IQ), conscientiousness (EQ), influence (EQ), and managing resources (MQ). Particularly low are competencies in the more strategic dimensions and in emotional resilience. Interviews and answers to the questionnaire did not identify particular dimensions correlated with project performance.

Renewal projects

Renewal projects require a balance of EQ, MQ, and IQ competencies. Although conscientiousness and sensitivity are required as EQ competencies, it is empowering and managing resources in the area of MQ competencies, as well as critical thinking and strategic perspective as IQ competency, that are required to the strongest extent. Self-awareness (EQ) and communication (MQ) were identified as being especially related to project performance. With these dimensions being low in the profile, it is indicated that much performance improvement could be achieved by developing these competencies to the next higher level.

The profile for renewal projects differs from that for IT projects in only one competency, the level of strategic perspective (IQ), renewal projects requiring high strategic perspective and IT projects just medium. We assume this means that most IT projects have the nature of renewal projects, but in IT projects the linking of the project to the strategy of the parent organization falls more on other governance roles such as the project sponsor, whereas in renewal projects that responsibility falls more on the project manager. For both,

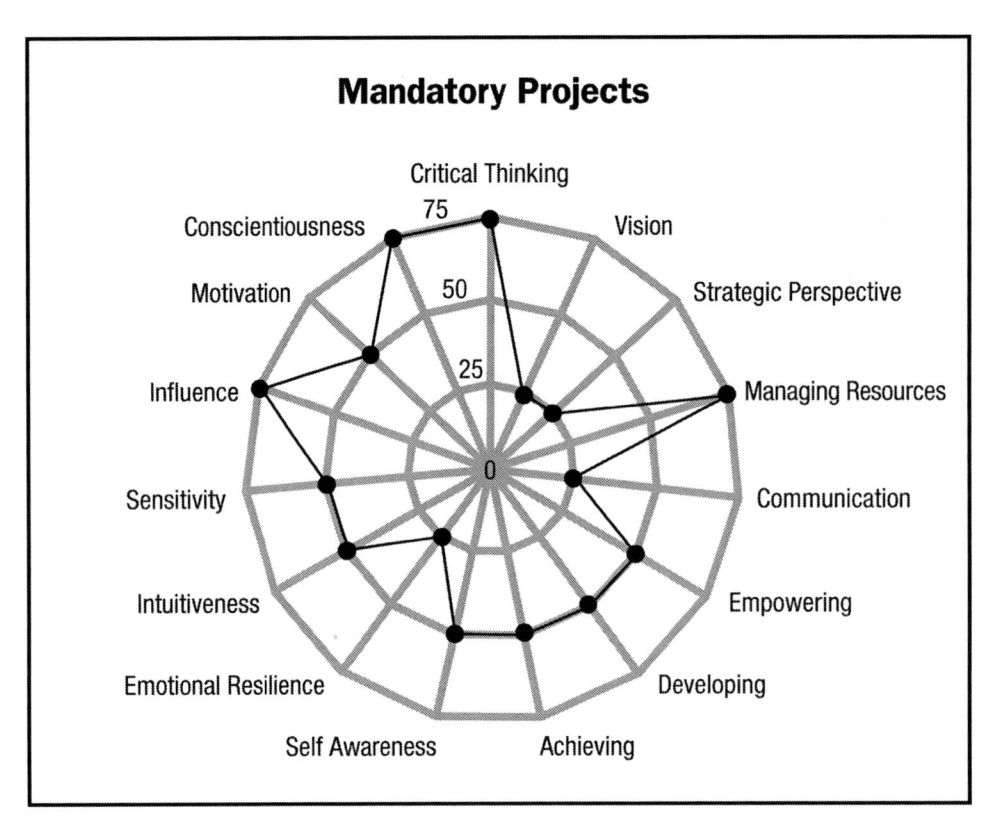

Figure 7-7   Project manager profile on high-performing, mandatory projects

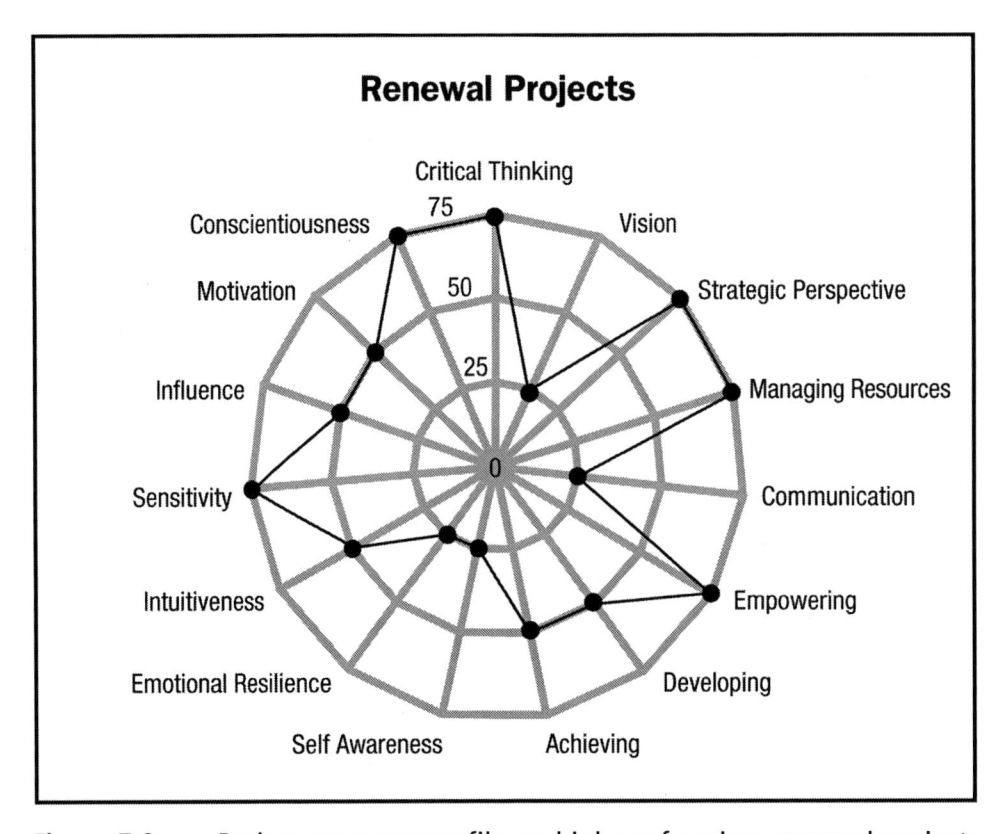

Figure 7-8   Project manager profile on high-performing, renewal projects

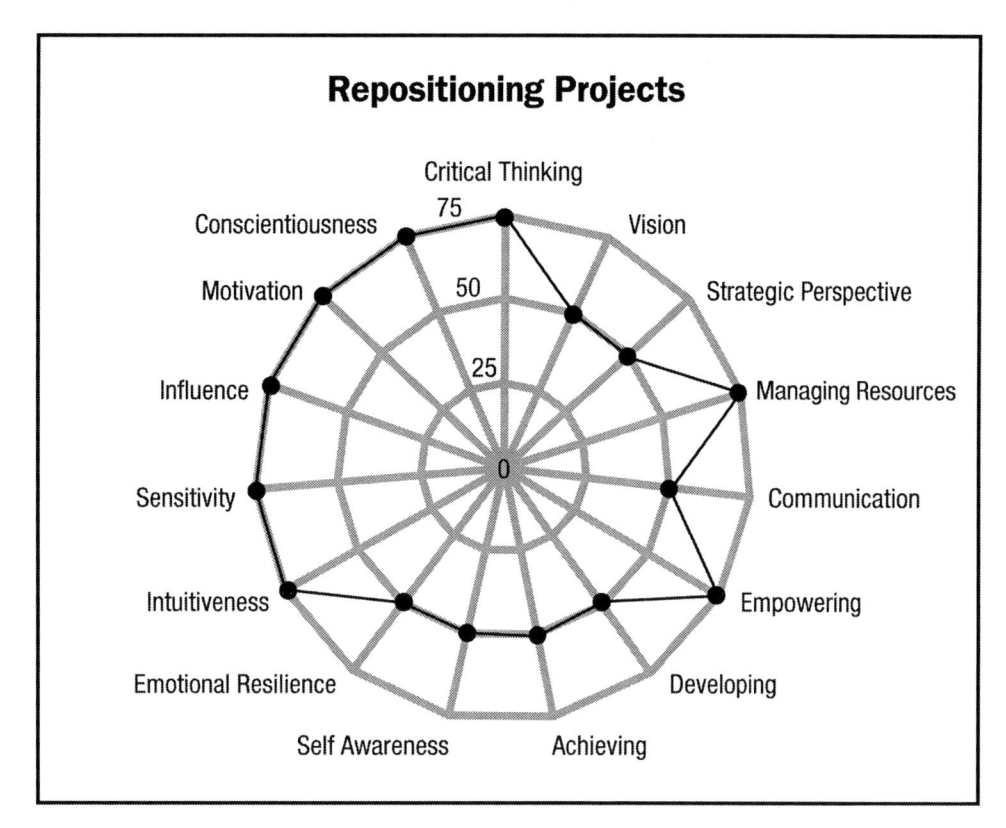

Figure 7-9   Project manager profile on high-performing, repositioning projects

vision (IQ) is low, meaning the project manager must be proactive in maintaining the link with the parent organization's strategy, but must not be active in setting the strategy.

Repositioning projects

Repositioning projects require strong emotional competencies, as well as empowering (MQ), managing resources (MQ), and critical thinking (IQ) competencies. Motivation (EQ) was identified in the interviews and on the questionnaire as being correlated with project performance. In accordance with the profile it requires strong motivation competencies to improve project performance even further.

Repositioning projects have a very similar profile to organizational change projects. Perhaps they are just two ways of saying the same thing, so it is encouraging that the profiles are similar. The managers of organizational change projects scored higher on vision but lower on critical thinking. Both therefore seem to have a role in setting organizational strategy, which would make sense for the managers of organizational change.

Comparison

Figures 7-7 to 7-9 illustrate an increasing need for stronger managerial competencies when moving from mandatory to renewal projects, and then the increase in emotional competencies when moving from renewal to repositioning projects.

Profiles by contract type

Figures 7-10 to 7-12 show the profiles of project managers in high performance projects with alliance, remeasurement, and fixed-price contract, respectively.

Alliance projects

The requirements stemming from alliance contracts are managed using conscientiousness (EQ) and influence (EQ). Dimensions for the management of self and others are medium strong and the more strategic

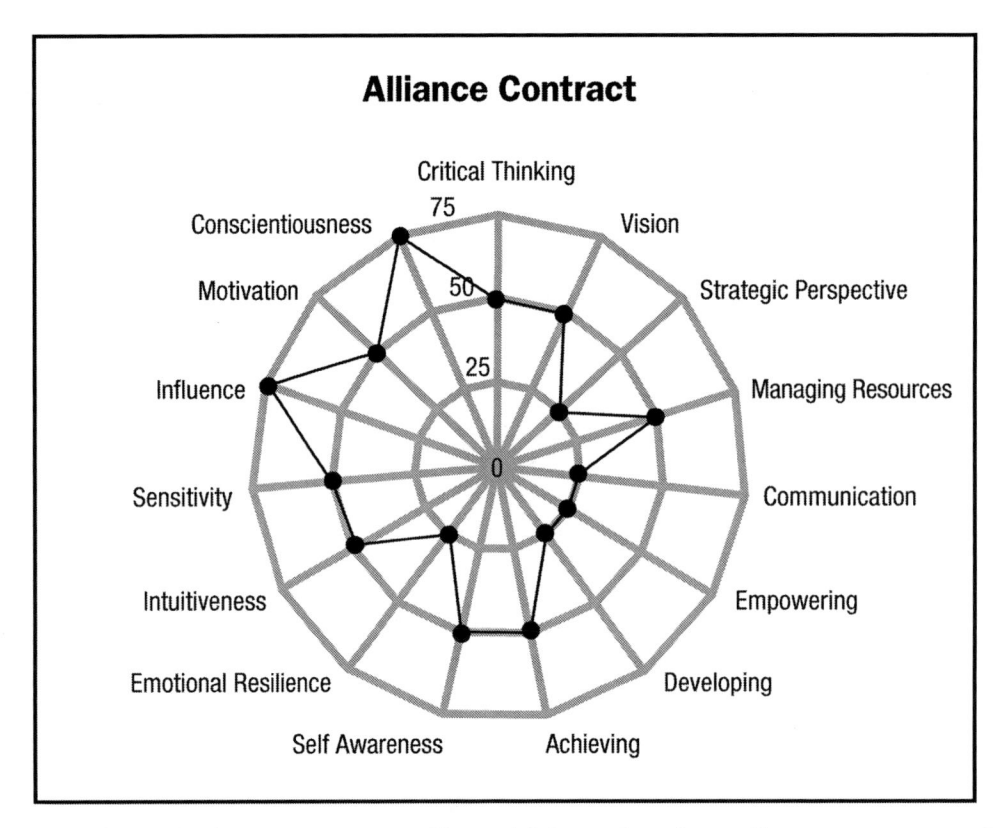

Figure 7-10   Project manager profile on high-performing, alliance contract projects

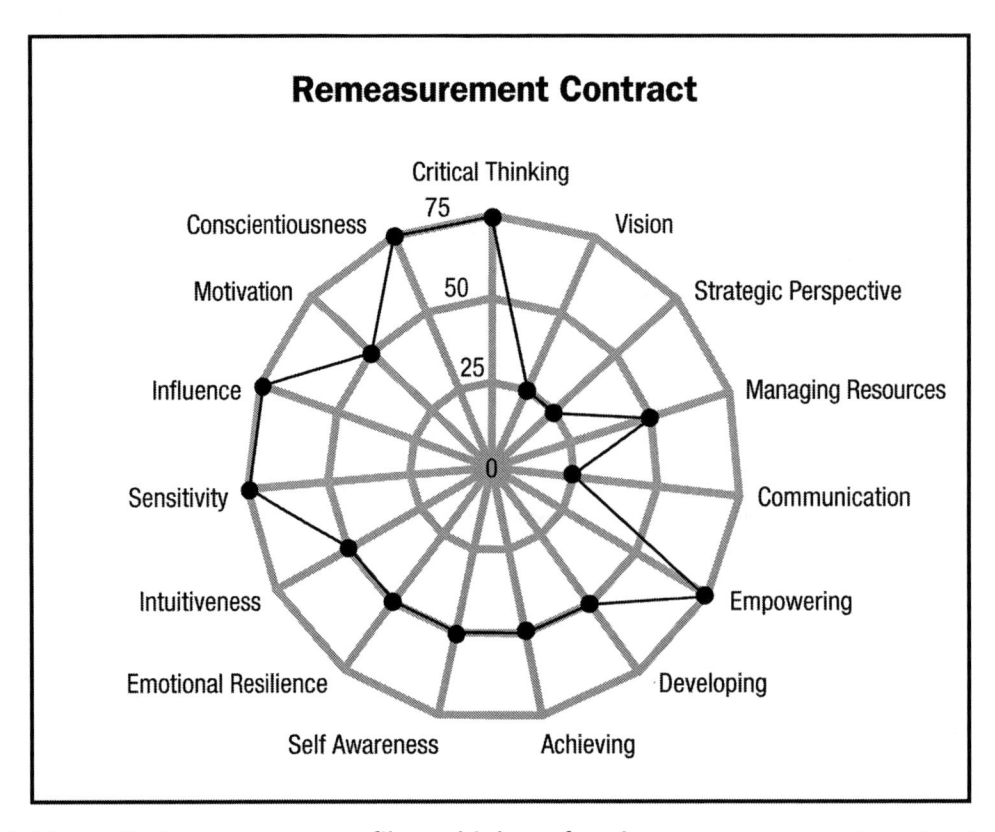

Figure 7-11   Project manager profile on high-performing, remeasurement contract projects

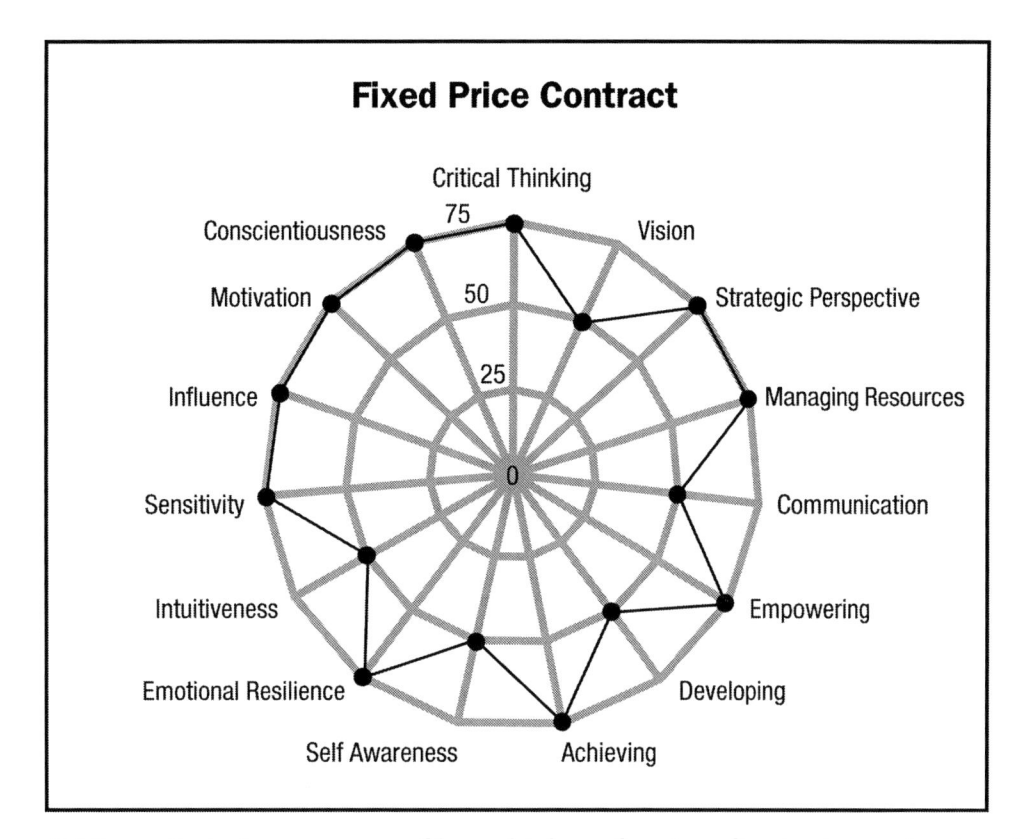

Figure 7-12   Project manager profile on high-performing, fixed-price contract projects

dimensions are low. The interviews and questionnaire answers did not give an indication which particular dimensions are correlated with project performance.

Remeasurement contracts

In addition to the strongest dimensions in projects with alliance contracts, projects based on remeasurement contract require empowerment (MQ), sensitivity (EQ), and critical thinking (IQ). More managerial competencies are required in these projects. Influence (EQ) and communication (MQ) were identified as being related with project performance. Increasing competencies in these dimensions will yield best results for project performance.

Fixed-price contracts

Managers of high-performing, fixed-price projects show strong competencies in most of the fifteen dimensions, especially in the EQ dimensions. Sensitivity (EQ) and communication (MQ) were identified as being correlated with project performance. The objective is therefore to develop project managers for these projects to peak level in sensitivity and medium levels of communication.

Comparison

Figures 7-10 to 7-12 show the increasing requirement for stronger-developed competencies as managers move from projects with alliance contracts, to remeasurement contracts and finally fixed-price contracts.

Profiles by life-cycle stage

Figures 7-13 to 7-16 show the profiles of project managers assigned to manage increasingly larger parts of the project life cycle. The figures show the profile of managers managing the following stages in a project:
- Figure 7-13: design, execution, and close-out
- Figure 7-14: design, execution, close-out, and commissioning
- Figure 7-15: feasibility, design, execution, and close-out
- Figure 7-16: feasibility, design, execution, close-out, and commissioning

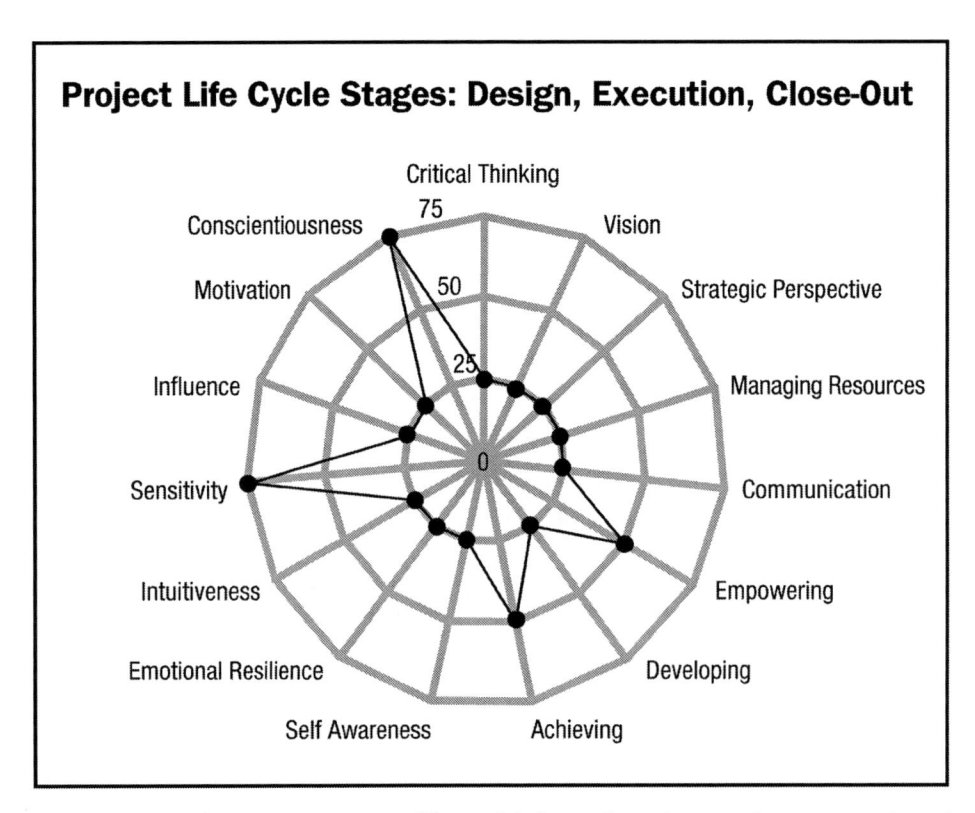

Figure 7-13   Project manager profile on high-performing projects, covering design, execution, and close-out stages

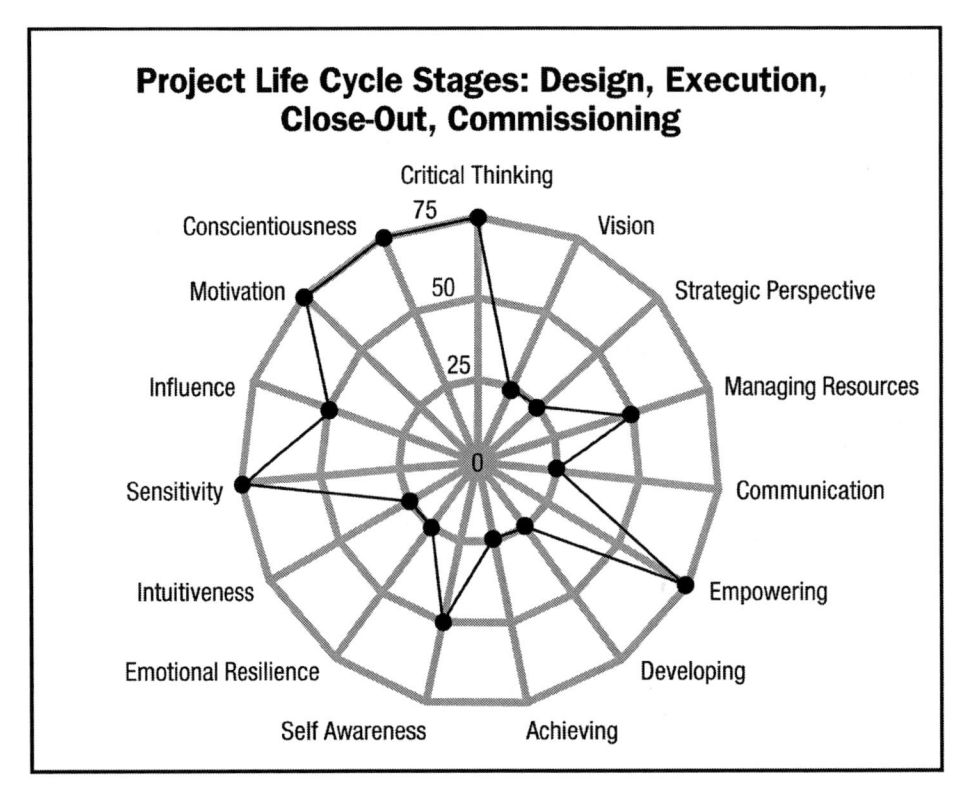

Figure 7-14   Project manager profile on high-performing projects, covering design, execution, close-out, and commissioning stages

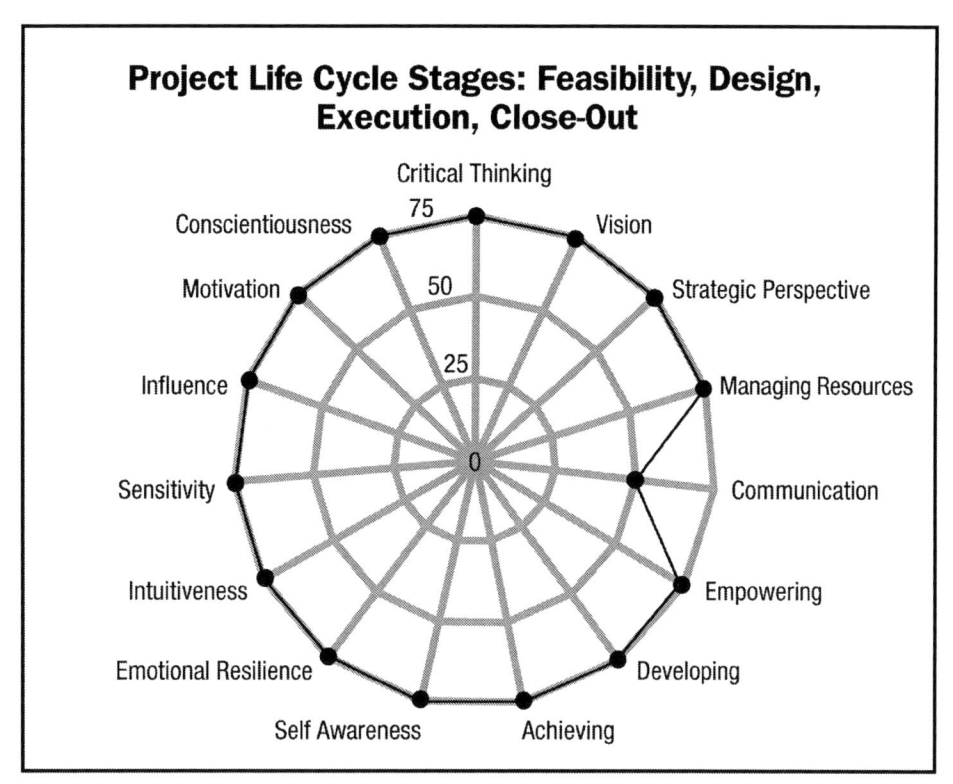

Figure 7-15   Project manager profile on high-performing projects, covering feasibility, design, execution, and close-out stages

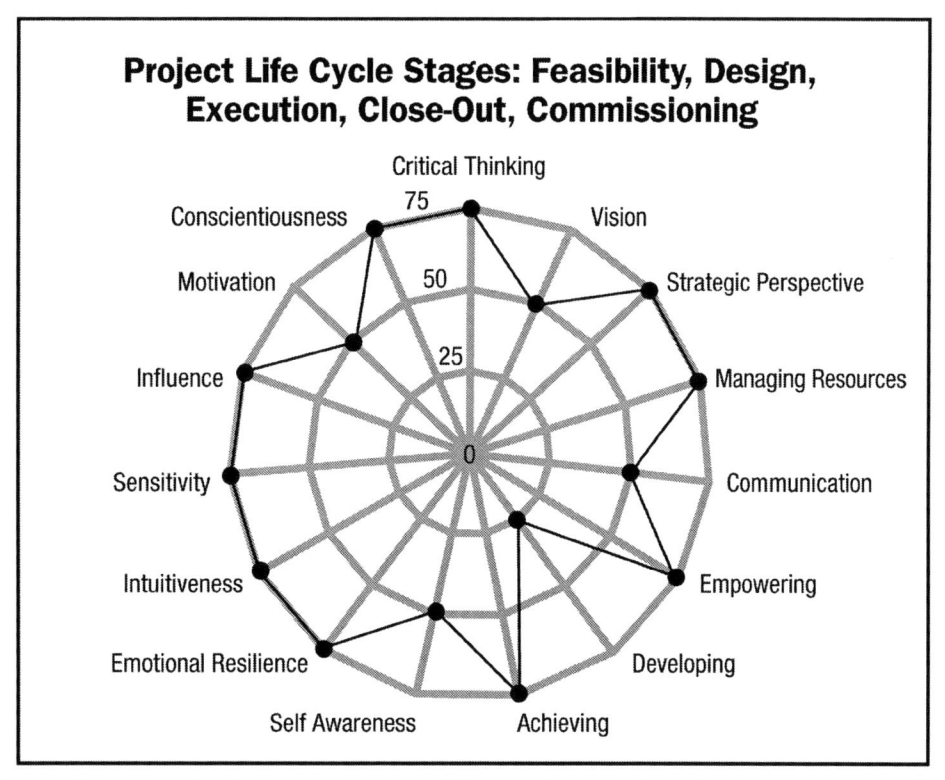

Figure 7-16   Project manager profile on high-performing projects, covering feasibility, design, execution, close-out, and commissioning stages

Design, execution, and close-out

Managing the design, execution, and close-out stages of a high-performing project require strong competencies in conscientiousness (EQ) and sensitivity (EQ). It shows the dependence of project results on EQ dimensions. Achieving (MQ) and empowering (MQ) are required to a medium extent. All other dimensions are only required to a low extent. Dimension identified as being related to project performance are conscientiousness and communication.

Design, execution, close-out, and commissioning

Managers covering the commissioning stage in addition to the three kernel stages previously described, show additional strong competencies in motivation (EQ), empowerment (MQ), and critical thinking (IQ). The commissioning stage, therefore, seems to require additional competencies not required to the same extent in the three kernel phases of a project. Motivation, sensitivity, and conscientiousness were also identified as those dimensions important for project performance.

Feasibility, design, execution, and close-out

Project managers in the feasibility, design, execution, and close-out of high performance projects show strongest competencies in all dimensions, except communication (medium strong). Very different from the profile of managers in the three kernel stages of a project, these project managers are all-round talents with highly developed competencies. The interviews and questionnaire showed that especially communication (MQ) and conscientiousness (EQ) are most important for performance in these project life cycles. Strategic perspective should not be executed to a larger extent by these project managers.

Feasibility, design, execution, close-out, and commissioning

Project managers covering all stages of a project, namely feasibility, design, execution, close-out, and commissioning show medium to high levels in all competencies, except for developing others (MQ). Dimensions identified as related with project performance (in addition to those for the three kernel stages) are motivation (EQ), conscientiousness (EQ), and sensitivity (EQ) for the commissioning stage.

Comparison

Looking at the four figures in the order just described shows an increasing balance of the three competencies (EQ, MQ, and IQ) together with in increase in the strength of each dimension, when expanding the focus of project management from design, execution, and close-out to the adjacent stages for feasibility and commissioning.

Chapter 8

Recommendations and Conclusions

In this chapter we present our recommendations and conclusions. We return to our research questions and hypotheses to recall the answers we have achieved to them. We then discuss the practical implications of these results for the managers the managers of project managers, and the theoretical implications for researchers into project leadership. Finally, we return to the two beliefs pervading the project management community and discuss the implications for the project management community as a whole.

Research questions and hypotheses

In Chapter 1, we presented two research questions for our research project:
1. Does the project manager's competence, including his or her leadership style, influence project success?
2. Are different competence profiles, including different leadership styles, appropriate for different types of project?

We defined "competence" as knowledge, skills, and, personal characteristics in achieving performance in a job as defined by appropriate standards. The general management literature has identified that it is the third of these dimensions that differentiates an effective leader from a good manager. Particularly, it has identified that it is leadership style, which in itself is primarily based on emotional intelligence, which mainly contributes to his or her performance as a manager and leader, and the performance of the organization being managed. The general management literature has also identified that different leadership styles are appropriate in different circumstances, in different types of organizations. We have suggested that it would be strange indeed if the same did not apply in the temporary organization that is a project. We therefore set out to show that it is the project manager's leadership style that influences his or her performance as a project leader, and the performance of the project being managed. We also set out to show that different leadership styles were appropriate on different types of projects.

In Chapter 4, we converted the two research questions into two hypotheses:

Hypothesis 1: The project manager's competency, which includes his or her leadership style, is positively correlated to project success.
Hypothesis 2: Different combinations of project management competency are correlated with success on different types of projects.

Through our interviews and Web-based questionnaire, we found that these two hypotheses were supported. From the general management literature, we identified a fifteen-dimensional model of leadership style, and from the project management literature and our interviews, we identified a ten-dimensional model of project success. Using those definitions of project success and leadership style, we showed that some of the fifteen dimensions of leadership style were correlated to project success. Thus, Hypothesis 1 was supported. From the project management literature we also identified different ways of categorizing projects. Based on that and our interviews, we adopted a simplified project categorization model, with six project attributes and nineteen categories of projects within those attributes. Using that model of project types, we found that on different project categories, different leadership competencies were correlated with project performance and different competencies had an impact on performance in different types of projects. Further, we were also able to identify the profiles of project managers of high-performing projects against the fifteen leadership competencies for seventeen of the nineteen different types of projects. Different profiles were appropriate for different types of projects. Thus, we concluded that Hypothesis 2 was supported.

Having concluded that the two hypotheses were supported, we were able to answer our two research questions in the affirmative.

1. The project manager's competence, including his or her leadership style, does influence project success. We have only looked at the third dimension of competence, the personal characteristics, particularly leadership style and emotional intelligence. We have shown those are correlated to project success. Other dimensions of competence, knowledge and skills, may or may not be correlated with project success. We have not looked at those. We direct you to Crawford (2001, 2003, 2005). We have shown that leadership style and emotional intelligence are significant differentiators of performance on projects, but we have not shown they are the main differentiators (but we believe they are).
2. Different profiles of competence, particularly different profiles of leadership style are appropriate on different types of projects. Again, we have only looked at the third dimension of competence, personal characteristics, and found that this does differentiate performance on different types of projects. We have not looked at knowledge and skills, and cannot say that personal characteristics are the main differentiator of performance, on different types of projects, just that they are significant.

Practical implications

So what are the practical implications of these results for the managers of project managers? There are two main suggestions:

1. When appointing project managers to projects you need to take into account their leadership style and make sure it is appropriate for the type of project they have to manage.
2. When developing project managers for the pool of potential project managers, you must ensure not only that you develop appropriate technical knowledge and skills for the projects they have to manage, but also appropriate personal characteristics. These include social skills, leadership style, and emotional intelligence. These need to be taken account of when managers are appointed to the pool and as they are developed within the pool.a

There are two associated implications for this second conclusion:

- Organizations need ways of assessing their project managers' leadership styles, when they are first appointed to the role, and at their annual appraisals, to identify their current style and determining programs to enhance desired characteristics.
- Organizations need to build into training and development programs modules to develop the desired emotional and managerial dimensions of leadership style for their types of projects.

To achieve this we suggest organizations adopt a five-step process:

Step 1: Recognize the types of projects the organization undertakes, and the appropriate leadership styles for those types of projects. A categorization system such as that suggested by Crawford, Hobbs, and Turner (2005) can be used.

Step 2: Assess the leadership styles of project managers in the project management pool. The leadership styles can be assessed at appointment and during the annual appraisal process. Tools such as the leadership development questionnaire (LDQ), developed by Dulewicz and Higgs (2005) can be used to assess leadership styles. (Anybody wishing to use the LDQ can contact the authors in the first instance. The authors' contact details are in Appendix A.)

Step 3: Develop those areas that are correlated with project performance for the types of projects undertaken by the organization. This can be achieved by adopting appropriate training programs, and by giving potential project managers experience on the relevant types of projects. By identifying where an individual project manager has weaknesses can help him or her focus on those areas of development.

Step 4: Maintain the profiles of individual project managers centrally, and choose appropriate project managers when projects are resourced.

Step 5: Value your project managers.

Theoretical implications

There are also three theoretical implications of our results.
1. Consistently with the general management literature (Goleman, Boyatzis, and McKee 2002; Dulewicz and Higgs 2003), we have identified the emotional dimensions of leadership as making the most significant contribution to project performance. This was not universally the case for all project types. On less complex projects, the managerial dimensions were sometimes more significant. But on the majority of project types, and always on the more complex ones, the emotional dimensions made the most significant contributions.
2. This leads into the second finding. With increasing project requirements, however measured (complexity, project type, duration of the life cycle, etc.), there is an increasing need for emotional competencies in the manager. Thus, transactional leadership, and concern for process, is more important on simple projects, but transformational leadership, and concern for people, is necessary on medium to high-complexity projects.
3. We identified that sometimes two project types require similar competency profiles in their managers. Sometimes the reason why is fairly obvious (e.g., in the case of organizational change and repositioning projects). Other times it is less obvious as in the case of IT and renewal projects. Similar profiles were required by the following pairs of project types:
   - IT projects and renewal projects
   - organizational change and repositioning projects
   - high-complexity projects, fixed-price projects and projects covering the feasibility, design, execution, and close-out stages of the project.

IT projects and medium-complexity projects also have the same profile for the emotional (EQ) and intellectual (IQ) dimensions of competence, but different ones for the managerial dimensions.

Further research may be needed to understand why these similarities exist.

Implications for the project management community

At the start of Chapter 1, we said there are two beliefs pervading the project management community.
1. The project manager's competence makes no contribution to project success. As long as he or she uses the right tools and techniques the project will be successful. The project success literature almost studiously ignores the project manager.
2. As long as a project manager has learned to apply those tools and techniques well, he or she can apply them to any type of project, regardless of technology, discipline, or domain.

On the other hand, we have seen that both of these beliefs are wrong.
1. The third dimension of competence, the project manager's personal characteristics, including leadership style and emotional intelligence, does make a contribution to project success.
2. Different profiles of that third dimension, different leadership styles, are required for better project performance on different types of project.

However, we would not write off all previous research as wrong, or even that the beliefs are totally misguided.
1. The previous research has tended to focus on the first two dimensions of competence, knowledge and skills. It is a complaint about the project management literature that it has tended to focus on the tools and techniques (Jugdev and Müller, 2005), to have shown a greater concern for process than for people. The general management literature has shown that knowledge and skills are not the most significant differentiators for managerial performance. Yes, a manager needs to have an entry level of knowledge and skills to perform as a manager. But once they have the entry-level knowledge and skills—more does not make them better. It is emotional intelligence that makes them better. Thus, if you only focus on the use of appropriate tools and techniques, you will find that the project manager's competence makes little contribution. You only see what you measure.
2. The same basic set of tools and techniques may be appropriate for all types of projects; one project management body of knowledge is right for all types of project. Crawford, Hobbs, and Turner (2005) showed that one reason for categorizing projects was to choose appropriate project management methodologies for the types of projects being undertaken by the organization. But it is not as if radically different bodies of knowledge will be used. It is different subsets of the one body of knowledge that will be used, and a different emphasis will be given to the elements used, depending on the types of projects. But the tools and techniques used will be drawn from one body of knowledge. Thus, if a

project manager has learned the tools and techniques in the body of knowledge, they can apply them to all types of project, as they know which subsets to use and the appropriate emphasis to give.

A project manager can manage any type of project; but performance will be impaired on some project types if the project manager doesn't change his or her leadership style. The general management literature suggests people can adapt their leadership style (within constraints imposed by their personality) (Goleman, Boyatzis, and McKee 2002). That is why we chose to focus on leadership style and not personality. So as an individual's career develops, he or she must look to enhance his or her leadership style. As he or she progresses from a junior project manager to a middle project manager to a senior project manager, he or she will progress from managing low-complexity projects to medium-complexity projects to high-complexity projects. So as he or she progresses he or she will need to enhance his or her leadership competencies, particularly developing the emotional dimensions. But also his or her vision must go from low, on low-complexity projects, focus on the task at hand, to high on high-complexity projects, worry about whether the change being undertaken delivers the parent organization's strategic objectives.

Thus, it is critical for organizations to measure their project managers' leadership competencies as part of the annual appraisal process and help project managers develop an appropriate profile for the projects they will manage in the future.

APPENDIX A

Author Contact Details

The authors can be contacted at:

Professor J Rodney Turner
Groupe ESC Lille
Avenue WillyBrandt
F59777 Euralille
France
Tel: +33-3-2021 5972
Fax: +33-3-2021 5974
E-Mail: jr.turner@esc-lille.fr

Dr. Ralf Müller
Umeå School of Business
Umeå University
901 87 Umeå
Sweden
Tel: +46-(0)40-68-91-312
Fax: +46-(0)40-68-91-312
E-mail: ralf.mueller@usbe.umu.se

Appendix B

Fifteen Competency Dimensions of Leadership

The fifteen leadership competencies are described by Dulewicz and Higgs as follows:

Emotional Competencies (EQ)

Self-awareness: Aware of one's own feelings and able to recognize and control them.

Emotional Resilience: Capability for consistent performance in a range of situations. Retain focus on a course of action or need for results in the face of personal challenge or criticism.

Intuitiveness: Arrive at clear decisions and drive their implementation in the face of incomplete or ambiguous information by using both rational and "emotional" perceptions.

Interpersonal Sensitivity: Be aware of, and take account of, the needs and perceptions of others in arriving at decisions and proposing solutions to problems and challenges.

Influence: Capability to persuade others to change a viewpoint based on the understanding of their position and the recognition of the need to listen to this perspective and provide a rationale for change.

Motivation: Drive and energy to achieve clear results and make an impact.

Conscientiousness: Capability to display clear commitment to a course of action in the face of challenge and to match "words and deeds" in encouraging others to support the chosen direction.

Managerial Competencies (MQ)

Resource Management: Organizes resources and coordinates them efficiently and effectively. Establishes clear objectives. Converts long-term goals into action plans.

Engaging Communication: Engages others and wins their support through communication tailored for each audience. Is approachable and accessible.

Empowering: Gives direct reports autonomy and encourages them to take on challenges, to solve problems, and develop their own accountability.

Developing: Encourages others to take on ever more-demanding tasks, roles, and accountabilities. Develops others' competencies and invests time and effort in coaching them.

Achieving: Shows an unwavering determination to achieve objectives and implement decisions.

Intellectual Competencies (IQ)

Critical Analysis and Judgment: Gathering relevant information from a wide range of sources, probing the facts, identifying advantages and disadvantages. Sound judgments and decision-making, awareness of the impact of any assumptions made.

Vision and Imagination: Imaginative and innovative. Having a clear vision of the future and foresee the impact of changes on implementation issues and business realities.

Strategic Perspective: Sees the wider issues and broader implications. Balances short- and long-term considerations and identifies opportunities and threats.

APPENDIX C

Project Categories

Attribute	Categories under that attribute	Subcategories	Previously used by:
1. Application area or product of the project	Engineering Information and technology Organizational change		Crawford (2002)
2. Stage of the product or project life cycle	Project life cycle	Concept Feasibility Design Execution Commissioning Operation Decommissioning	
	Product life cycle	Research Development Launch Manufacture	
	Product portfolio	Problem child Rising star Cash cow Dog	Clarke and Pratt (1985)
3. Project size and groupings	Project portfolio Programs Major project Single project		
4. Strategic importance	Survival Renewal Repositioning		BP
5. Strategic positioning	Time critical Cost critical Quality critical Process critical Relationship critical		
6. Geography	International Domestic	Home client, foreign contractor Foreign client, home contractor Foreign client, foreign contractor Single site, multi-site	

(continued)

7. Project scope	Single function Several functions Several companies Several industries		
8. Project timing	Regular Fast build Fast track Concurrency		
9. Ambiguity, familiarity	Runners Repeaters Strangers Aliens		
10. Risk	Likelihood of failure Consequence of failure Impact of risk Location of risk Type of risk	Business, insurable Internal, external	
11. Complexity	Stable Change Transformation		Dulewicz and Higgs (2003)
12. Customer, supplier relations	Internal customer External customer Internal supplier External supplier		
13. Ownership, funding	Parent company—revenue Parent company—capital Limited recourse financing Project financing		
14. Type of contract	By scope of supply	Work package Design Build Design and build Turnkey Concession Prime contract	
	By management responsibility	Construction management Management contracting Design-procure-build	
	By terms of payment	Cost plus Remeasurement Fixed price	
	Alliance	Target price	

Table C-1   Project categories after Crawford, Hobbs, and Turner (2005)

APPENDIX D

Interview Questions

Nature of the company

1. Tell me about the nature of the company:
   - What sort of work is done in the company?
   - What is the management philosophy of the company?
   - What is the size and number of projects undertaken?
   - What sorts of projects are undertaken?
   - What categories of projects are undertaken (compared with Table D-1)?
   - What is the project management maturity of the organization (scale from 1 = low to 5 = high)?

Project success

2. How do you define project success?
   - Does your definition of success influence your choice of project manager?

Project manager's personality style and project type

3. Is the project manager's personality style independent of the project type?
   - Are project managers in your organization more people- or task-orientated?
   - Why?
   - Is that appropriate?
   - What are the personality characteristics important for your project managers?
   - Why?
   - Can you grade the importance of the fifteen personality characteristics in Table D-2 for your project managers?

Selecting project managers

4. Does the project type make a difference in selecting project managers?
   4.1 Is there a range of types of projects (five project type dimensions)?
   4.2 Do you think you are looking for different types of project managers on different projects?
   4.3 Do you think there are other dimensions to the project type that are important?

Anything else

5. Is there anything else that impacts the style of project manager you are looking for?

Application	Complexity	Life-cycle stage	Strategic importance	Culture
Engineering	Stable	Concept	Survival	Domestic
IT	Change	Feasibility	Renewal	Host
Organizational Change	Transformation	Design	Repositioning	Ex-patriot
		Execution		
Commissioning				

Table D-1   Categories of project types

Competency	Not important	Low	Medium	High
1. Critical analysis and judgment				
2. Vision and imagination				
3. Strategic perspective				
4. Engaging communication				
5. Managing resources				
6. Empowering				
7. Developing				
8. Achieving				
9. Emotional				
10. Self-awareness				
11. Emotional resilience				
12. Motivation				
13. Sensitivity				
14. Influence				
15. Intuitiveness				
16. Conscientiousness				

Table D-2   Relative importance of importance of the project manager's characteristics

APPENDIX E

Interview Data

This appendix contains information about the companies we interviewed. We interviewed fourteen people from several companies.

Company information

Table E-1 contains information about the companies the fourteen interviewees work for. It shows:
- The nature of the company
- The country it is located in
- The job title of the interviewee
- The number of staff
- The ownership
- The nature of the work
- The interviewees assessment of the maturity of the company

Ownership of the firm was not a question asked, but was identified by some interviewees as significant in their selection of project managers. Particularly, three from privately owned companies said that maintaining long-term relationships with customers was more important than year-on-year profit growth, and that required a different type of project manager.

Nature of projects undertaken

Table E-2 contains information about the nature of the projects undertaken.
Table E-3 shows the attributes of the projects undertaken as identified by the interviewees.

Project success

Table E-4 shows how the interviewees said their organizations judge project success.

Selecting project managers

Table E-5 shows the criteria mentioned by the interviewees for selecting project managers.
Table E-6 shows whether the interviewees thought their project managers were task-focused or people-focused.
Table E-7 shows the interviewees' ratings of the leadership competencies in choosing project managers.

No.	Nature of Company	Country	Title of Interviewee	No. of Staff	Ownership	Nature of Work	Project Maturity
1	Project Management Consultancy	Australia	Managing Director	95	Owned by directors	40% expert witness 40% specialist project management 20% strategic consulting	High
2	Project Management Consultancy	France	Director	15–18	French operation of UK firm	Contract management Project management Specialist project services	High
3	Project Management Consultancy	Holland	Consultant	100	Subsidiary of IT consultancy	Project management Project consultants on government projects	4
4	Project Management Consultancy	Germany	Manager Professional Services	100	Subsidiary of US firm (as 5 & 6)	Consulting services Information systems for data warehousing	3–4
5	Project Management Consultancy	U.K.	Executive Program Manager	120	Subsidiary of US firm (as 4 & 6)	Consulting Project management Specialist project services	Medium
6	Project Management Consultancy	USA	Vice President Professional Services	100	Subsidiary of U.S. firm (as 4 & 5)	Consulting Project management Specialist project services	High
7	Design, IS and Innovation Consultancy to car industry	Sweden	Program Director	1,600 (world)	Swedish Parent	Design and development Information handling Innovation management	High (5)
8	Design and Construction Engineers	France	Commercial Director	2,000	Family owned (perennité)	Mechanical contractor Small design office Green and brown field	High

(continued)

No.	Nature of Company	Country	Title of Interviewee	No. of Staff	Ownership	Nature of Work	Project Maturity
9	Telephone Operator	Austria	Project Manager	10,000 (parent)	Division of large firm	IT/IS projects in accounts Department of national telephone operating company	4
10	Telephone Operator	Austria	Project Controller	10,000 (parent)	Division of large firm	Product development projects for national telephone operating company	High
11	Mobile Telephone Operator	Sweden	Business Projects Large Accounts	18	Department	Internet services for businesses and private customers for mobile telephone operating company	4
12	Mobile Telephone Operator	Sweden	Business Development	60	Project office	Efficiency and effectiveness improvement projects for mobile telephone operating company	3
13	Airline Operator	Austria	Project Manager	4,500 (parent)	Project office	Reorganization, IS/IT, marketing and construction projects for national air carrier	3
14	Manufacturer of Integrated Packing and Distribution	Sweden	Director of Product Development	100	Product development department	Premium: value added packaging Value: volume, quality, low cost Emerging: new markets	3–4

Table E-1   Organizations interviewed

No.	No. of Projects	Typical Duration	Nature of Projects	Size of Projects min/median/max
1	50 at a time 200 per year	1 months-2 years	80% Construction: (Building, Infrastructure, Engineering) 20% Telecoms	Aus $20 million/ Aus $50 million/ Aus $1 billion
2	15–20 at a time	1–2 years	Building, infrastructure process plant Foreign companies in France French companies overseas	€10 million plus
3	100 at a time	6 months–1 year	Infrastructure Urban renewal	—
4	60 at a time	6 months	Integrated consultancy, software and hardware design Database design and implementation	—
5	15 at a time	Up to 2 years	Data warehouse solutions Start-up: Design, development, training Roll-out	—
6	Single program 3 years long	3 year program	Organizational redesign, process improvement, IT infrastructure, change management	—
7	20 at a time	2 years	Development of new models Design improvement	—
8		1–2 years	Mechanical construction Green field sites (new plant) Brown field sites (revamp and retrofit)	€3 million/ -/ €200 million
9	2 at a time (interviewee)	1 year	IS/IT projects: SAP implementation, archiving system, electronic billing, internet payment system	€1.5 million
10	2 at a time (interviewee)	—	Internal: change, IS/IT, process change External: new products	Complexity more significant
11	35–50 at a time	—	Systems integration R&D	€1 million/ €4 million/
12	30 at a time	—	Voice recognition, internal shipments employee well-being	—
13	70 at a time	6 months	IS/IT, construction Marketing, new destinations, Reorganization,	€100,000/ €500,000/ €750,000
14	30 at a time	16–24 months	Product development	—

Table E-2   Nature of projects in the organizations interviewed

Company / Attribute		1	2	3	4	5
Application area	• E&C • ICT • Business	Main business Telecoms A little with AMP	Main business Part of building None	Main business — —	None Main business Linked	None Yes Yes
Difficulty	• Simple • Medium • Complex	No No Nature of business	Not required Yes Yes	— — Main business	None Main business Some	None Yes Yes
Life cycle	• Concept • Feasibility • Design • Execution • Close-out • Post-closure	Yes Yes Yes Yes Yes Litigation	Sometimes Sometimes Not often Main business Part of execution	Yes Yes Yes Yes Yes	Main business Main business Main business Main business Main business	Yes Yes Yes Yes Yes
Strategic importance	• Survival • Renewal • Repositioning	Olympic work Some Main business	Asbestos cleaning Refurbishment New facilities	— Main business —	35%–40% 25% 35%–40%	No Yes No
Culture	• Domestic • Foreign at home • Ex-patriot	Main business Some Some	Some Yes Yes	Mainly — —	70% — 30%	No No Yes
Contract type	• Fixed price • Alliance • Remeasurement	Yes Some Yes	Yes Yes Yes			

Table E-3   Attributes of projects undertaken by the organizations interviewed

(continued)

Company / Attribute		6	7	8	9
Application area	• E&C • ICT • Business	None Yes Yes	Main business None None	Main business None None	None Main business Some
Difficulty	• Simple • Medium • Complex	None Yes Yes	None Main business Some	Green field Green field/revamp Revamp	None None Main complex, several departments
Life cycle	• Concept • Feasibility • Design • Execution • Close-out • Post-closure	Yes Yes Yes Yes Yes	Main business Main business Main business Main business Main business	Sometimes/alliance Not often Not often Main business Part of execution	1st step design process 2nd step design IT system, (IT Dept) 3rd step implement
Strategic importance	• Survival • Renewal • Repositioning	No Yes No	Some Main business Some	Environmental Maintenance Greenfield/revamp	Paperless billing, consolidation Archiving Electronic billing, internet payment
Culture	• Domestic • Foreign at home • Ex-patriot	No No Yes	Projects Customers —	Mainly Some	Mainly domestic Subsidiaries
Contract type	• Fixed price • Alliance • Remeasurement			LSTK Yes	

Table E-3   Attributes of projects undertaken by the organizations interviewed

(continued)

Company / Attribute		10	11	12	13	14
Application area	• E&C • ICT • Business	None ICT Business process	None Main business Some	None Some Main business	Construction IT Infrastructure Reorganization	Main business None None
Difficulty	• Simple • Medium • Complex	A B C	None Some Main business	None Main business Some	Task force Standard project Grand project	Some Main business Rarely
Life cycle	• Concept • Feasibility • Design • Execution • Close-out • Post-closure	Evaluations Rest as 9	Often Main business Main business Main business Main business	Main business Main business Main business Main business Main business	Pure conceptual Concept and realization Realization Part of realization	Main business Main business Main business Main business Main business
Strategic importance	• Survival • Renewal • Repositioning	Sarbanes-Oxley Efficiency products Internet over TV	None Main business None	Main business Main business None	Legal changes Building, ICT New destinations	Main business None None
Culture	• Domestic • Foreign at home • Ex-patriot	Internal Subsidiaries	Some Some Some	Main business Some Some	Parent Local subsidiary Foreign subsidiary	Some Main business None
Contract type	• Fixed price • Alliance • Remeasurement					

Table E-3   Attributes of projects undertaken by the organizations interviewed

No.	Criteria for judging project success
1	The client keeps coming back.
2	Satisfied client (only the interviewee's client is important; it does not matter how the client's client feels).
3	Impact on the environment of the project stakeholders. Value is added in the most efficient way.
4	Achieving scope, time and budget (in that order of priority). Follow on business.
5	Satisfied client. Achieving functionality and other performance indicators defined. Performance indicators usually linked to strategy.
6	Deliver promised benefits. Achieve time, cost, and functionality. Satisfied stakeholders.
7	Achieve key economic measures. Achieve customers defined success criteria. (No correlation between line and project organizations' measures of success.)
8	Satisfaction of stakeholders, client, subcontractors, own staff. The client keeps coming back. Achieve safety and quality.
9	Achieve defined objectives.
10	Achieve defined objectives. Achieve time and cost.
11	Satisfied client. Achieve time. Minimize disruption. Satisfy sales department.
12	Achieve cost and time (in that order of priority). Timely response to unexpected events. Achieve prioritization of project in whole organizations so adequate resources are made available.
13	Achieve goals.
14	Achieve time and cost (in that order of priority).

Table E-4   How the interviewees judged project success

Company	1	2	3	4	5
Criteria for selecting project managers for a given project	Able to deal with stakeholders • Different stakeholders need different personalities • Ability to communicate with relevant stakeholders Type of contract • Fixed price: gung-ho, focused on time and cost • Remeasurment: technical, sensitive, trustworthy, calm, logical, honest on progress	Able to deal with complexity Able to work with client Skill in relationships Language Technical competence Form of contract Ethics and morals	Subject knowledge Political sensitivity (snq)* Form of assignment • Consultancy: ability to manage resources Project management: focus on outcomes	Form of contract Duration Internal/external awareness Political sensitivity Nature of client Expected issues: • personal drive • motivational • sells future business • details versus big picture	Competency profile (snq) Able to communicate Able to plan Forceful Motivated, self-starter
Is leadership style a factor in choosing project managers?	Always	Said not per se But gave examples that contradicted this	Yes	Yes, especially Presence Self-confidant, assertive Sees opportunities, not problems Holistic understanding of situation Flexibility to change Balance of tough and soft	Only on large projects
What constitutes a complex project if a criterion for selection?	Size Stakeholders Form of contract	Some clients Some geographies Form of contract	—	—	Large projects
Note: snq (sine non qua): Entry ticket qualification project managers must have. It is not a criterion for choosing someone to manage a particular project, but a criterion for choosing someone to join the pool of potential project managers.					

Table E-5   Criteria mentioned by the interviewees for selecting project managers

(continued)

Company	6	7	8	9	10
Criteria for selecting project managers for a given project	Domain knowledge Project management skills Personality Flexibility	Relationship with customer Social capabilities Fit with organization	Length of experience Technical competence Form of contract Geography Able to negotiate (snq)	Experience Education and competence Department Location and nature of work	Leadership skills Competence Able to deal with ambiguity Able to deal with emotions • fear, aggression • conflict Able to communicate On large, complex projects • self-confident • stable • tolerant
Is leadership style a factor in choosing project managers?	Yes, especially: • results orientation • discipline in approach • balancing objectives • attention to detail • persuasiveness • negotiation	Yes, especially: • problem solving • business orientations • ability to identify opportunities • self-awareness • learns from mistakes	Only on complex projects Fast track, alliance, revamp Not Greenfield, alliance Fast track requires • reactivity • stabilityAlliance requires • good at relationships • able to understand others • able to accept criticism	No	Yes, see above
What constitutes a complex project if it is a criterion for selection?	—	—	Fast track Alliancing Some geographies	—	Size Number of departments
Note: snq (sine non qua): Entry ticket qualification project managers must have. It is not a criterion for choosing someone to manage a particular project, but a criterion for choosing someone to join the pool of potential project managers.					

Table E-5   Criteria mentioned by the interviewees for selecting project managers

(continued)

Company	11	12	13	14
Criteria for selecting project managers for a given project	Experience and prior education Fit with this customer Opinion of sales Able to deal with customers (snq) • presence • management experience Achieve balance between work and home life (snq)	Experience Competence Interest in that project Fit of knowledge with requirements Fit with other project participants Development opportunity Confidence in using project management techniques Impact on private life	Project management knowledge Experience and training Familiar with project type Business knowledge Familiar with business process Department Able to cope with change	Project complexity Expected issues, conflicts Number of resources Level of top management attention Experience Duration and budget Availability of resources Able to speak English (snq)
Is leadership style a factor in choosing project managers?	Yes, see above	Yes, especially: • drive, self-confidence • independence • sharp, sensitive • self-awareness • able to multi-task • able to delegate • able to deal with conflict • diplomatic, leadership • able to communicate • work in project culture	Yes, especially: • self-confidant • holistic view • systematic view • perception of things and point of things • organic view • able to work through interfaces	Yes, especially • structured • organized • straight forward • energetic • positive attitude • able to stand in front of top management • able to delegate • decision making • able to prioritize
What constitutes a complex project if it is a criterion for selection?	—	—	Size (over €500,000).	Complexity Expected issues Resources required
Note: snq (sine non qua): Entry ticket qualification project managers must have. It is not a criterion for choosing someone to manage a particular project, but a criterion for choosing someone to join the pool of potential project managers.					

Table E-5   Criteria mentioned by the interviewees for selecting project managers

No.	Task versus people orientation of project managers
1	Both are important. People are promoted for being people-oriented but also for achieving project success. Team working is important. Being able to maintain the team is a contributory factor.
2	People-oriented project managers more likely to achieve project success.
3	Try to achieve a balance.
4	Task-oriented project managers more likely to achieve project success.
5	Tend to be people-focused. Technical competence taken as a given.
6	Both.
7	60% task oriented, 40% people oriented. Project manager needs to focus on the task, line manager on the people.
8	In France project managers need to be people-oriented (see 2).
9	Both. Need to understand impact of emotions.
10	Leadership skills and technical skills both important.
11	People-oriented project managers more likely to achieve project success.
12	Project managers who are both people-oriented and task-oriented are more likely to achieve project success.
13	Try to encourage project managers to be people-oriented. But a fundamental transformation takes place on appointment as a project manager.
14	Project managers who are both people-oriented and task-oriented are more likely to achieve project success.

Table E-6   Task versus people orientation of project managers

Leadership competency	Rate	Average Group	Average Competency	1	2	3	4	5	6	7	8	9	10	11	12	13	14
Intellectual competencies		2.1															
1. Critical analysis and judgment	M		2.5	2	2	2	3	3	2	2	3	2	3	2	3	3	2
2. Vision and imagination	L		1.9	2	2	2	2	1	2	3	1	2	2	2	2	2	2
3. Strategic perspective	L		2.0	1	3	1	2	2	2	2	1	2	3	3	2	2	2
Managerial competencies		2.4															
4. Engaging communication	M		2.5	3	2	3	3	3	3	1	2	2	3	3	2	2	2
5. Managing resources	H		2.6	1	3	2	3	2	3	3	3	3	2	2	3	3	3
6. Empowering	H		2.4	1	2	2	2	3	2	2	3	3	3	3	2	3	3
7. Developing	L		2.0	2	2	1	1	1	2	2	n	3	3	2	2	3	3
8. Achieving	H		2.7	1	3	3	3	3	2	3	3	3	3	3	2	3	3
Emotional competencies		2.4															
9. Self-awareness	M		2.4	2	2	3	2	2	2	2	3	3	2	2	3	3	3
10. Emotional resilience	M		2.4	2	1	3	3	2	3	1	3	2	2	3	2	3	2
11. Motivation	H		2.7	3	3	3	3	2	3	2	2	3	3	3	3	3	3
12. Sensitivity	M		2.4	3	2	3	2	2	2	2	3	3	3	2	2	3	3
13. Influence	M		2.4	2	1	2	3	3	2	2	3	3	2	3	2	2	3
14. Intuitiveness	L		2.0	3	3	2	2	2	2	2	2	3	2	2	1	3	2
15. Conscientiousness	M		2.5	2	2	1	3	3	2	3	3	2	3	3	2	3	2

Table E-7   Rating of the leadership competencies of project managers

APPENDIX F

Web-based Questionnaire

What follows in Part 1 of the Web-based questionnaire. We are unable to include Part 2 because that is proprietary to Henley Management College.

Leadership Style and Project Success
This PMI supported research project investigates the question whether the competence of the project manager, including personality and leadership style, is a success factor on projects.

A) - Project types
The following questions ask about the types of projects you manage. Please click on those categories that best represent your project

PT01: My last project was of the following type ...
Please choose the appropriate response for each item
- Engineering ☐ Yes ☐ Uncertain ☐ No
- Information Technology / Information Systems ☐ Yes ☐ Uncertain ☐ No
- Business or organizational change ☐ Yes ☐ Uncertain ☐ No

PT02: My last project was of the following complexity ...
Please choose **only one** of the following:
- ☐ High
- ☐ Medium
- ☐ Low

PT03: In my last project I managed the following stages of the project life-cycle ...
Please choose **all** that apply
- ☐ Feasibility
- ☐ Design
- ☐ Execution & Control
- ☐ Close-out
- ☐ Commissioning

PT04: My last project was of the following strategic importance ...
Please choose **all** that apply
- ☐ Mandatory (a project required e.g. by law)
- ☐ Repositioning (e.g. a project for entirely new products or services)
- ☐ Renewal (e.g. further development of an existing system)

PT05: In my last project I worked ...
Please choose **only one** of the following:
- ☐ in my home country
- ☐ on a project outside my home country
- ☐ abroad as an expatriate

PT06: My last project was based on the following contract type ...
Please choose **only one** of the following:
- ☐ Fixed-price
- ☐ Remeasurement (e.g. cost reimbursement, time & material etc.)
- ☐ Alliance

B) - Project success
The following questions ask about how you measured success and how successful the project was.

SU01: In my last project, the following factors were important for overall project success ...
Please choose the appropriate response to each item

	Not at all important	Not important	Slightly important	Important	Very important
Client satisfaction with project results	☐	☐	☐	☐	☐
Reoccuring business with this client	☐	☐	☐	☐	☐
End-user satisfaction with project product or service	☐	☐	☐	☐	☐
Suppliers satisfaction	☐	☐	☐	☐	☐
Project team's satisfaction	☐	☐	☐	☐	☐
Other stakeholders' satisfaction with the project	☐	☐	☐	☐	☐

SU02: Another main factor that determined success in my project was (please specify):
Please write your answer here:

SU03: How important was the factor you just entered for project success:
Please choose **only one** of the following:
☐ Not all important
☐ Not important
☐ Slightly important
☐ Important
☐ Very important

SU04: Please give your opinion about the results of your last project.
Please choose the appropriate response for each item

	Disagree	Slightly disagree	Neither agree nor disagree	Slightly agree	Agree
Altogether, the project performed well in terms of functionality, budget and timing.	☐	☐	☐	☐	☐
The project met the users requirements.	☐	☐	☐	☐	☐
The project achieved its purpose.	☐	☐	☐	☐	☐

SU05: My last project was successful in terms of ...
Please choose the appropriate response for each item

	Disagree	Slightly disagree	Neither agree nor disagree	Slightly agree	Agree
Client satisfaction with project results	☐	☐	☐	☐	☐
Reoccuring business with this client	☐	☐	☐	☐	☐
End-user satisfaction with project product or service	☐	☐	☐	☐	☐
Suppliers' satisfaction	☐	☐	☐	☐	☐
Project team's satisfaction	☐	☐	☐	☐	☐
Other stakeholders' satisfaction with the project	☐	☐	☐	☐	☐
Your own success factor you entered above	☐	☐	☐	☐	☐

C) - Demographics

DE01: Your name (must be the same as in the second part of the questionnaire):
Please write your answer here:

DE02: Are you a certified project manager:
Please choose **only one** of the following:
☐ Yes
☐ No

DE04: Please enter your email address here, in case you would like to receive a summary of the research results.
Please write your answer here:

D) - Competencies
You enter now the second part of the questionnaire.

: The next screen asks you to submit your answers for the first part of the questionnaire. After that you are presented a web-link to the second part of the survey. Please click on that web-link to continue with the survey. Thank you.

Submit Your Survey
Thank you for completing this survey. Please fax your completed survey to: +46 (0)90 - 786 66 7 by 2005-12-18.

APPENDIX G

Web-based Questionnaire Data and Analysis

This appendix contains data from the Web-based questionnaire.

Sample demographics

The number of responses to the Web-based questionnaire totaled 415, of which 400 could be used for further analysis. Fifteen of the responses to the two questionnaires could not be reconciled. Of the 400 responses:

1. **Gender:** 262 were male (66%) and 138 female (34%).
2. **Industry Sector:** 272 responses were from the private sector (68%), 110 from the public sector (28%), and 18 from not-for-profit organizations (5%).
3. **Age:** the mean age was 45.7 years, with a standard deviation of 8.5 years.
4. **Job function:** Table G-1 shows job function. The largest number of respondents held technical positions (43%), followed by general management positions (19%), and R&D positions (7%). Other functions each accounted for 5% or less.
5. **Geography:** Table G-2 shows the respondents' country. The largest number of respondents were from North America (56%), followed by Europe (21%). All other countries were represented in the remainder (23%).
6. **Professional qualifications:** Table G-3 shows the respondents' levels of professional qualification. Sixty-six percent said they were certified project managers, 33% non-certified, and 1% did not respond to the question.

Missing values were kept at a minimum because the Web questionnaires required answers to almost all questions. One respondent did not answer the questions on project performance.

Response bias was tested by comparing responses from the first week after the questionnaire launch with responses from the last week. No significant differences ($p \leq .05$) were found. Responses peaked in week two

Job Function	Frequency	Percent
General Management	74	19%
Marketing/Sales	13	3%
HRM/Training	6	2%
Finance	6	2%
R & D	27	7%
Manufacturing	18	5%
Technical	171	43%
Other	86	22%
Total	400	100%

Table G-1   Sample demographics by job function

Nationality	Frequency	Percent
North America	224	56%
Europe	84	21%
Other	92	23%
Total	400	100%

Table G-2   Sample demographics by nationality

Certified	Frequency	Percent
Yes	263	66%
No	132	33%
No response	5	1%
Total	400	100%

Table G-3   Sample demographics by project management certification

with 50% of all answers, compared to 34% in week one, 10% in week three, and 6% in week four (see Figure G-1).

Table G-4 shows the score for the fifteen leadership competencies across the sample. On average the EQ dimensions for intuitiveness were lowest relative to the other dimensions. Conscientiousness and self-awareness were highest among the 400 respondents.

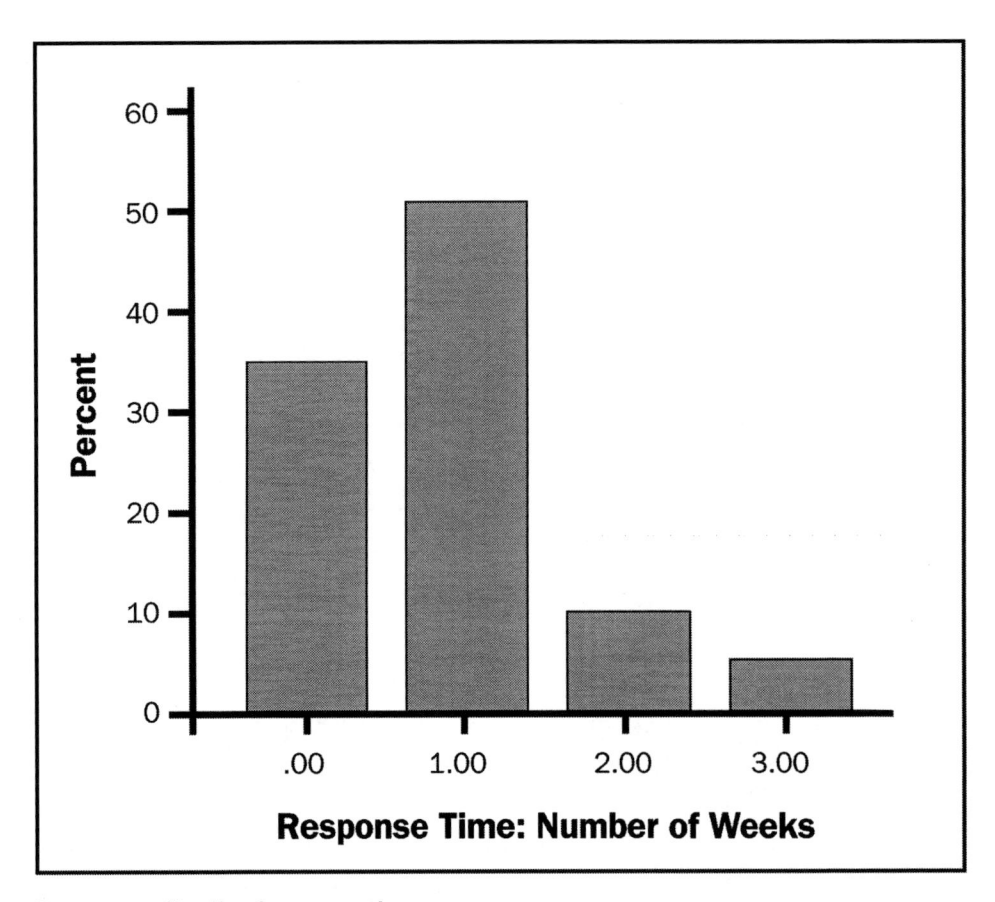

Figure G-1   Response distribution over time

Competency	N	Minimum	Maximum	Mean	Std Deviation
EQ-motivation	400	28	48	38.74	3.576
EQ-conscientiousness	400	31	50	42.68	3.432
EQ-sensitivity	400	31	50	42.21	3.507
EQ-influence	400	26	46	37.44	3.367
EQ-self-awareness	400	30	50	42.61	3.522
EQ-emotional resilience	400	25	48	37.51	4.054
EQ-intuitiveness	400	19	46	32.95	4.741
MQ-managing resources	400	25	50	40.64	3.960
MQ-communication	400	29	50	41.24	4.117
MQ-developing	400	21	50	40.17	4.635
MQ-empowering	400	26	48	39.43	3.606
MQ-achieving	400	28	48	36.87	3.261
IQ-strategic perspective	400	30	50	39.77	3.814
IQ-vision	400	23	49	36.28	4.296
IQ-critical thinking	400	30	50	41.28	3.630
Valid N (list-wise)	400				

Table G-4 Data descriptions of the fifteen competencies

Quantitative analysis of questionnaire data

Step 1 of the quantitative analysis started with the creation of summary variables for EQ, MQ, and IQ, and performance.

The variable for EQ was created from the average of the mean values of the seven underlying dimensions for self-awareness, emotional resilience, motivation, sensitivity, influence, intuitiveness, and conscientiousness. A Cronbach alpha value of .77 indicates good reliability of the data.

The MQ variable was calculated as the average from the mean values of engaging communication, managing resources, empowering, developing, and achieving. A Cronbach alpha of .88 indicates high reliability.

The IQ variable was calculated as the average of the mean values for critical analysis and judgment, vision and imagination, as well as strategic perspective. Again, a Cronbach alpha of .83 showed very reliable data.

The performance variable was calculated as the average of the mean values of all ten success variables, which were as follows:
- Overall assessment of performance against time, cost, and quality
- Meeting user requirements
- Achieving the project's purpose
- Client satisfaction with the results
- Reoccurring business with the client
- End-user satisfaction with the project outcome
- Supplier's satisfaction
- Project team's satisfaction
- Other stakeholder's satisfaction
- Achievement of other, self-determined, success criteria

A Cronbach alpha of .87 showed also high reliability of the responses.

In order to distinguish between low and high-performing projects, the performance variable was used to create a categorical variable (lohi_perf) by splitting performance at the mean (see Table G-5). Projects at or above the variable's mean of 4.4332 were classified as high performing (257 projects), and those under the variable's mean were classified as low performing (142 projects).

The descriptions of the variables created are shown in Table G-5. EQ has the smallest range; its lowest values are higher than the other two competencies. However, its mean is lower than that of IQ and MQ.

	N	Minimum	Maximum	Mean	Std Deviation
EQ	400	31.57	45.86	39.1614	2.43629
MQ	400	27.60	48.40	39.6690	3.24314
IQ	400	30.33	48.67	39.1058	3.38821
Perform	399	1.20	5.00	4.4332	0.64546
Valid N (listwise)	399				

Table G-5   Data descriptions of the calculated variables

In accordance with the research model we used stepwise multivariate regression analysis techniques to assesses the correlation between the competence dimensions (as independent variables) and project performance (as dependent variable), for each type of project (as moderator variable).

Regressions were done in two stages:
1. We assessed the correlation of the three summary dimensions of EQ, MQ, and IQ with project success.
2. We used the fifteen underlying competencies and assessed their correlation with project performance. That allowed for increasing level of granularity and a stepwise understanding of the different relationships in different project types.

Regressions of the EQ, MQ, and IQ competencies against performance showed that EQ becomes increasingly important in high-performing projects. This is in line with the results from the qualitative study, where interviewees said that personality of the project manager is only important in projects of higher complexity.

Validation

The approach and steps used for validation are described in Chapter 3. As a first step we used the interviewee scores on the fifteen competency dimensions to calculate the scores for the three project types engineering, IT, and organizational change projects. The results are shown in Tables G-6 to G-8, respectively. Here, engineering projects scored lowest on IQ, while organizational change projects scored lowest on EQ and MQ. IT projects scored highest in all three dimensions. Dimensions ranked as high or medium in the interviews were mapped against the dimensions identified as significantly correlated with performance through the questionnaire. Those dimensions that fit both criteria, and whose underlying sample size was sufficient to warrant conclusions, were identified as validated dimensions of importance for project performance.

Leadership competency	Rate	Average Group	Average Competency	1	2	3	7	8	13	14
Intellectual competencies		2.0								
4. Critical analysis and judgment	M		2.3	2	2	2	2	3	3	2
5. Vision and imagination	L		2.0	2	2	2	3	1	2	2
6. Strategic perspective	L		1.7	1	3	1	2	1	2	2
Managerial competencies		2.4								
9. Engaging communication	M		2.1	3	2	3	1	2	2	2
10. Managing resources	H		2.6	1	3	2	3	3	3	3
11. Empowering	H		2.3	1	2	2	2	3	3	3
12. Developing	L		2.2	2	2	1	2	n	3	3
13. Achieving	H		2.7	1	3	3	3	3	3	3
Emotional competencies		2.4								
16. Self-awareness	M		2.6	2	2	3	2	3	3	3
17. Emotional resilience	M		2.1	2	1	3	1	3	3	2
18. Motivation	H		2.6	3	3	3	2	2	3	2
19. Sensitivity	M		2.7	3	2	3	2	3	3	3
20. Influence	M		2.1	2	1	2	2	3	2	3
21. Intuitiveness	L		2.1	3	1	2	2	2	3	2
22. Conscientiousness	M		2.3	2	2	1	3	3	3	2

Table G-6   Interviewee ratings of competencies, engineering projects

Leadership competency	Rate	Average Group	Average Competency	4	5	9	10	11
Intellectual competencies		2.3						
7. Critical analysis and judgment	M		2.6	3	3	2	3	2
8. Vision and imagination	L		1.8	2	1	2	2	2
9. Strategic perspective	L		2.4	2	2	2	3	3
Managerial competencies		2.6						
14. Engaging communication	M		2.8	3	3	2	3	3
15. Managing resources	H		2.4	3	2	3	2	2
16. Empowering	H		2.8	2	3	3	3	3
17. Developing	L		2.0	1	1	3	3	2
18. Achieving	H		3.0	3	3	3	3	3
Emotional competencies		2.5						
23. Self-awareness	M		2.2	2	2	3	2	2
24. Emotional resilience	M		2.4	3	2	2	2	3
25. Motivation	H		2.6	3	2	2	3	3
26. Sensitivity	M		2.4	2	2	3	3	2
27. Influence	M		2.8	3	3	3	2	3
28. Intuitiveness	L		2.0	2	2	2	2	2
29. Conscientiousness	M		2.8	3	3	2	3	3

Table G-7   Interviewee ratings of competencies, IT projects

Leadership competency	Rate	Average Group	Average Competency	6	12
Intellectual competencies		2.2			
10. Critical analysis and judgment	M		2.5	2	3
11. Vision and imagination	L		2.0	2	2
12. Strategic perspective	L		2.0	2	2
Managerial competencies		2.3			
19. Engaging communication	M		2.5	3	2
20. Managing resources	H		3.0	3	3
21. Empowering	H		2.0	2	2
22. Developing	L		2.0	2	2
23. Achieving	H		2.0	2	2
Emotional competencies		2.2			
30. Self-awareness	M		2.5	2	3
31. Emotional resilience	M		2.5	3	2
32. Motivation	H		3.0	3	3
33. Sensitivity	M		2.0	2	2
34. Influence	M		2.0	2	2
35. Intuitiveness	L		1.5	2	1
36. Conscientiousness	M		2.0	2	2

Table G-8   Interviewer ratings for organizational change projects

Project manager profiles on high performing projects

Finally, we sought to determine profiles against the fifteen competency dimensions of project managers from different types of high performing projects. It complements the work above, where we sought to identify those of the fifteen dimensions important for project success that is those which are correlated with performance. Now, we attempt to show to what extent each dimension is present in the managers of high performing projects of different types. This was done in several steps:

Identifying important competencies

A *t*-test was done to identify those competencies significantly more strongly developed in project managers of high performing projects than in low performing projects. The results showed all dimensions, except intuitiveness, are significantly higher (at $p = .05$) in high-performing projects. Intuitiveness appears to be unrelated with project success, but all other dimensions are more strongly developed within managers of high-performing projects.

Comparing project types

The next step in the analysis was to identify statistically significant differences within groups of projects; that is, between projects of different complexity, or between project with different contract types, etc. ANOVA analyses showed that perspective (IQ), emotional resilience (EQ), sensitivity (EQ), influence (EQ), and motivation (EQ) are significantly higher in high-complexity projects than in other projects (see Table G-9). It indicates a need for high emotional intelligence in complex projects.

Differences in the strength of the fifteen dimensions were also found between different life-cycle stages of projects. Project managers managing not only the kernel stages of design, execution, and close-out of a project, but also the feasibility and commissioning stages show significantly higher competencies in vision and managing resources than those managing the kernel stages only. Those managing the feasibility stage showed higher competencies in achieving (MQ), and those managing the commissioning stage showed higher levels of strategic perspective (IQ), when compared with project managers in kernel stages only. More details are shown in Table G-10.

Dimension	Significance (*p*) overall	Difference	Significance (*p*) of difference
EQ-emotional resilience	.006	1 > 2	.007
EQ-influential	.010	1 > 2	.012
EQ-motivation	.000	1 > 2 1 > 3	.003 .004
MQ-achieving	.025	1 > 2	.045
Key: 1 = high-complexity projects 2 = medium-complexity projects 3 = low-complexity projects			

Table G-9   Significant differences in high-performing projects of different complexity

Dimension	Significance (*p*) overall	Difference	Significance (*p*) of difference
IQ-visionary	.006	C > A D > A	.041 .012
IQ-perspective	.010	D > A	.042
MQ-managing resources	.022	D > A C > A	.029 .018
MQ-achieving	.006	C > A	.028
Key: A = Design, Execution, Close-out B = Design, Execution, Close-out, Commissioning C = Feasibility, Design, Execution, Close-out D = Feasibility, Design, Execution, Close-out, Commissioning			

Table G-10   Significant differences in high-performing projects at different project life-cycle stages

Looking at projects with different contract types, significant differences were found in the strength of empowering (MQ). Project managers in fixed-price and remeasurement contracts scored significantly higher than those in alliance contracts (Table G-11).

Normalizing scores

To identify the profiles of project managers in different types of projects the sample data were normalized and compared to normalized sample of managers developed by Dulewicz and Higgs (2003). Their normalized sample has a range of 1 to 10 for each competency dimension, with a mean of 5.5, and standard deviation of 2. The normalized scores are called *sten codes*. The normalized data of the project managers' sample showed a relatively homogeneous group of managers; none of the dimensions had a standard deviation that reached Dulewicz and Higgs's 2.0. Communication (MQ) and developing (MQ) scored lowest, with average sten codes of 5.21 and 5.27, respectively, and conscientiousness (EQ), critical analysis (IQ), and sensitivity (EQ) scored highest, with average sten codes of 6.09, 5.75 and 5.73, respectively, against an average of 5.5 for Dulewicz and Higgs's normalized data. The data descriptions of the sten codes for our sample are given in Table G-12.

Dimension	Significance (*p*) overall	Difference	Significance (*p*) of difference
MQ-empowering	.015	1 > 3	.016
		2 > 3	.048
Key: 1 = Fixed Price 2 = Remeasurement 3 = Alliance			

Table G-11   Significant differences in high-performing projects using different contract types

	Sten Scores			
	Min	Max	Mean	Standard Deviation
Critical Analysis	1	10	5.75	1.70
Vision	1	10	5.36	1.79
Perspective	1	10	5.49	1.75
Managing Resources	1	9	5.40	1.73
Self-awareness	1	9	5.46	1.70
Emotional Resilience	1	10	5.37	1.77
Intuitiveness	1	10	5.54	1.86
Sensitivity	1	10	5.73	1.70
Influencing	1	10	5.46	1.68
Communication	1	9	5.21	1.84
Empowering	1	10	5.61	1.78
Developing	1	9	5.27	1.85
Motivation	1	10	5.44	1.71
Achieving	1	10	5.52	1.55
Conscientiousness	1	10	6.09	1.73

Table G-12   Range, mean and standard deviation of sten codes from our sample

Individual profiles

We were then in a position to identify the individual profiles of project managers in high-performing projects of different type. We did this by first categorizing responses to the fifteen dimensions in high, medium and low, by selecting high-performing projects only and using the sten codes for identifying the particular profile of the fifteen dimensions in different types of projects. In accordance with Dulewicz and Higgs (2005), sten code values between 1 and 4 were categorized as low, those between 5 or 6 as medium, and 7 or higher as high. We then identified the profile of a project manager for each project type through identification of the particular strength in each dimension in high-performing projects. This was done by calculating the percentage of sten codes being low, medium or high for each dimension and each project type. The profile for a dimension for high-performing projects and all project types was then determined by assigning a profile level of low, medium or high. This was done by taking medium (sten code levels 5 and 6) as a basis, because it's the mean of sten codes for all dimensions. Profile levels were assigned:

- If less than 25% of the responses were in each of the categories low or high, the assigned profile level was medium
- If more than 25% of the sten codes in a dimension were classified as high then the overall profile level assigned was high (and low if more than 25% were in the low category).
- If both low and high categories had more than 25%, but were less than 5 percentage points apart, the profile level assigned was medium. Otherwise the more populated of the two categories was taken to assign a respective profile level of either low or high.

The results are described in Chapter 7.

References

Adair, J. 1983. *Effective Leadership: A Self-Development Manual.* Adershott, UK: Gower.
Alimo-Metcalfe, B., and R.J. Alban-Metcalfe. 2001. "Development of the TLQ." *Journal of Occupational & Organizational Psychology* 74, no 1: 1–24.
Andersen, E.S., K.V. Grude, T. Haug,, and J.R. Turner. 1987. *Goal Directed Project Management.* London, UK: Kogan Page/Coopers & Lybrand.
Antonakis, J., B.J. Avolio, and N. Sivasubramaniam. 2003. "Context and leadership: an examination of the nine-factor full-range leadership theory using the Multifactor Leadership Questionnaire." *The Leadership Quarterly* 14, no 3: 261–295.
Baker, B.N., P.C. Murphy, and D. Fisher. 1988. "Factors affecting project success." In *Project Management Handbook*, 2nd edition, edited by D.I. Cleland, and W.R. King. New York: Van Nostrand Reinhold.
Barnard, C.I. 1938. *The Functions of the Executive.* Cambridge, MA: Harvard University Press.
Bass, B.M. 1990. "From Transactional to Transformational Leadership: Learning to Share the Vision." *Organisational Dynamics* 18, no 3: 19–31.
Bass, B.M., and B. Avolio. 1995. *The Multifactor Leadership Questionnaire.* Palo Alto, CA: Mind Garden.
Belbin, R.M. 1986. *Management Teams.* London, UK: Heinemann.
Belout, A., and C. Gauvreau. 2004. "Factors Affecting Project Success: The Impact of Human Resource Management." *International Journal of Project Management* 22, no 1: 1–12.
Bennis, W. 1989. *On Becoming a Leader.* London, UK: Hutchinson.
Besner, C., and J.B. Hobbs. 2004. "An Empirical Investigation of Project Management Practice: In Reality, Which Tools Do Practitioners Use?" *Proceedings of PMI Research Conference 2004, London, July 11–14.* Newtown Square, PA: Project Management Institute.
Björkman, I., and A. Schaap. 1992. "Outsiders in the Middle Kingdom: Expatriate Managers in Chinese-Western Joint Ventures." *Journal of International Business Studies* 23, no 1: 55–75.
Blake, R.R., and S.J. Mouton. 1978. *The New Managerial Grid.* Houston, TX: Gulf.
Boyatsis, R.E. 1982. *The Competent Manager: A Model for Effective Performance.* New York: Wiley.
Briggs-Myers, I. 1992. Gifts Differing. Palo-Alto, CA: Consulting Psychologists Press.
Cattell, R.B., H.W. Eber, and M.M. Tatsuoka. 1970. *Handbook for the 16PF.* Illinois: IPAT.
Clarke, C., and S. Pratt. 1985. "Leadership's Four-Part Progress." *Management Today* (March): 84–86.
Collinson, D. 1998. *Fifty Major Philosophers.* London, UK: Routledge.
Collinson, D., K. Plan, and R. Wilkinson. 2000. *Fifty Eastern Thinkers.* London, UK: Routledge.
Cooke-Davies, T. 2001. "The 'Real' Project Success Factors." *International Journal of Project Management* 20, no 3: 185–190.
Covey, S.R. 1992. *Principle Centred Leadership.* New York: Fireside.
Crawford, L.H. 2001. *Project Management Competence: The Value of Standards.* DBA Thesis, Henley-on-Thames: Henley Management College.
Crawford, L.H. 2003. "Assessing and Developing the Project Management Competence of Individuals." In *People in Project Management*, edited by J.R. Turner. Aldershot, UK: Gower.
Crawford, L.H. 2005. "Senior Management Perceptions of Project Management Competence." *International Journal of Project Management* 23, no 1: 7–16.
Crawford, L.H., J.B. Hobbs, and J.R. Turner. 2005. *Project Categorization Systems: Aligning Capability with Strategy for Better Results.* Newtown Square, PA: Project Management Institute.
Dainty, A.R.J., M. Cjeng, and D.R. Moore. 2005. "Competency-based Model for Predicting Construction Project Managers' Performance." *Journal of Management in Engineering*, (January), 2–9.
Dulewicz, V. 1995. "A Validation of Belbin's Team Roles from 16PF & OPQ Using Bosses' Ratings of Competence." *Journal of Occupational & Organizational Psychology* 68, no 2.
Dulewicz, V., and M.J. Higgs. 2000. "Emotional Intelligence: A Review and Evaluation Study." *Journal of Managerial Psychology* 15, no 4: 341–368.

Dulewicz, V., and M.J. Higgs. 2003. "Design of a New Instrument to Assess Leadership Dimensions and Styles." *Henley Working Paper Series* HWP 0311, Henley-on-Thames, UK: Henley Management College.

Dulewicz, V., and M.J. Higgs. 2004. "Leadership dimensions questionnaire: organisation context, leader performance & follower commitment. *Henley Working Paper Research Note,* Henley-on-Thames, UK: Henley Management College.

Fiedler, F.E. 1967. *A Theory of Leadership Effectiveness.* New York: McGraw-Hill.

Frame, J.D. 1987. *Managing Projects in Organizations.* San Francisco: Jossey Bass.

Goffee, R., and G. Jones. 2000. "Why Should Anyone Be Led By You?" *Harvard Business Review* (Sept–Oct): 63–70.

Goleman, D., R. Boyatzis, and A. McKee. 2002. *The New Leaders.* Boston: Harvard Business School Press.

Hair, J., R.E. Anderson, R.L. Tatham, and W.C. Black. 1998. *Multivariate Data Analysis,* 5th edition. Prentice Hall.

Handy, C.B. 1982. *Understanding Organizations.* London, UK: Penguin.

Hartman, F., and R.A. Ashrafi. 2002. "Project Management in the Information Systems and Information Technologies Industries." *Project Management Journal* 33, no 3: 5–15.

Hastings, C., and W. Briner. 1996. "Coping with Cultural Differences." In *The Project Manager as Change Agent* edited by J.R. Turner, K.V. Grude, and L. Thurloway. London, UK: McGraw-Hill.

Hershey, P., and K.H. Blanchard. 1988. *Management of Organizational Behaviour,* 5th ed. Englewood Cliffs, NJ: Prentice Hall.

Hobbs, J.B., N. Pettersen, and H. Guérette. 2001. "Building, Validating and Implementing a PM Competency Model: The Experience of One Aerospace Company." In *Proceedings of the PMI Annual Symposium, Nashville, November 2001.* Newtown Square, PA: Project Management Institute.

Hofstede, G. 1991. *Cultures and Organizations: Software of the Mind.* London, UK: McGraw-Hill.

House, R.J. 1971. "A Path-Goal Theory of Leader Effectiveness." *Administrative Science Quarterly* (September): 321–338.

Judgev, K., and R. Müller. 2005. "Success is a Moving Target: A Retrospective Look at Project Success and Our Evolving Understanding of the Concept." *Project Management Journal* 36, no 4: 19–31.

Keegan, A.E., and D.N. Den Hartog. 2004. "Transformational Leadership in a Project-Based Environment: A Comparative Study of the Leadership Styles of Project Managers and Line Managers." *International Journal of Project Management* 22, no 8: 609–618.

Kendra, K., and L.J. Taplin. 2004., "Project Success: A Cultural Framework." *Project Management Journal* 35, no 1: 30–45.

Kets de Vries, M.F.R., and E. Florent-Treacy. 2002. "Global Leadership from A to Z: Creating High Commitment Organisations." *Organisation Dynamics* (Spring): 295–309.

Kirkpatrick, S.A., and E.A. Locke. 1991. "Leadership Traits Do Matter." *Academy of Management Executive* (March): 44–60.

Kloppenborg T.J., and J.A. Petrick. 1999. "Leadership in Project Life-Cycle and Team Character Development." *Project Management Journal* 30, no 2: 8–13.

Kotter, J.P. 1990. "What Leaders Really Do." *Harvard Business Review* (May–June): 37–60.

Kouznes, J.M., and B.Z. Posner. 1998. *Encouraging the Heart.* San Francisco: Jossey-Bass.

Krech, D., R.S. Crutchfield, and E.L. Ballachey. 1962. *Individual in Society.* New York: McGraw-Hill.

Lee-Kelley, L., K. Leong, and Loong. 2003. "Turner's Five Functions of Project-Based Management and Situational Leadership in IT Services Projects." *International Journal of Project Management* 21, no 8: 583–591.

Mäkilouko, M. 2004. "Coping with Multi-Cultural Projects: The Leadership Style of Finnish Project Managers." *International Journal of Project Management* 22, no 5: 387–396.

Margerison, M., and D. McCann. 1990. *Team Management.* Mercury Press.

Marshall, W. 1991. "Leaders into the '90s." *Personnel Journal* 70, no 5: 80–86.

Morris, P.W.G. 1988. "Managing Project Interfaces." In *Project Management Handbook,* 2nd Edition edited by D.I. Cleland and W.R. King. New York: Van Nostrand Reinhold.

Morris, P.W.G. 1997. *The Management of Projects,* 2nd Edition. London, UK: Thomas Telford.

Morris, P.W.G., and G. Hough. 1987. *The Anatomy of Major Projects: A Study of the Reality of Project Management.* Cichester: Wiley.

Müller, R., and J.R. Turner. 2004. "Cultural differences in Project Owner-Manager Communication." In *Innovations—Project Management Research 2004* edited by D.P. Slevin, D.I. Cleland, and J.K. Pinto. Newtown Square, PA: Project Management Institute.

Partington, D.A. 1997. PhD Thesis. Cranfield, UK: Cranfield University.

Partington, D.A. 2003 "Managing and Leading." In *People in Project Management* edited by J.R. Turner. Aldershott, UK: Gower.

Pinto, J.K., and J.E. Prescott. 1988. "Variations of Critical Success Factors over the Stages in the Project Life-Cycle." *Journal of Management* 14, no 1: 5–18.

Pinto, J.K., and D.P. Slevin. 1988. "Critical Success Factors in Effective Project Implementation." In *Project Management Handbook*, 2nd edition edited by D.I. Cleland and W.R. King. New York: Van Nostrand Reinhold.

Rees, D. 2003. "Managing Culture." In *People in Project Management* edited by J.R. Turner. Aldershot, UK: Gower.

Robbins, S.P. 1997. Essentials of Organizational Behaviour. Englewood Cliffs, NJ: Prentice Hall.

Rodrigues, C.A. 1988. "Identifying the Right Leader for the Right Situation. *Personnel* (September): 43–46.

Schultz, W.C. 1955. *FIRO: A Three Dimensional Theory of Interpersonal Behaviour.* New York: Holt, Rinehart, Winston.

Selmer, J. 2002. "Coping Strategies Applied by Western vs Overseas Chinese Business Expatriates in China." *International Journal of Human Resource Management* 13 no 1: 19–34.

Slevin, D.P. 1989. *The Whole Manager.* New York: Amacom.

Shenhar, A. 2001. "One Size does Not Fit All Projects: Exploring Classical Contingency Domains." *Management Science* 47, no 3: 394–414.

Tannenbaum, R., and K.H. Schmidt. 1958. "How to Choose a Leadership Style." *Harvard Business Review* (March–April).

Thamhain, H. 2004. "Linkages of Project Environment to Performance: Lessons for Team Leadership." *International Journal of Project Management* 22, no 7: 533–544.

Trompenaars, F. 1993. *Riding the Waves of Culture.* London, UK: Economist Books.

Turner, J.R. 1999. *The Handbook of Project-based Management: Improving the Processes for Achieving Strategic Objectives.* London, UK: McGraw-Hill.

Turner, J.R. 2004. *Managing Web Projects: The Management Large Projects and Programmes for Web-space Delivery.* Aldershott, UK: Gower

Turner, J.R., A.E. Keegan, and L.H. Crawford. 2003. "Delivering Improved Project Management Maturity Through Experiential Learning." In *People in Project Management* edited by J.R. Turner. Aldershot: Gower.

Turner, J.R., and R. Müller. 2003. "On the Nature of the Project as a Temporary Organization." *International Journal of Project Management* 21, no 1: 1–8.

Turner, J.R., and R. Müller. 2004. "Communication and Cooperation on Projects Between the Project Owner as Principal and the Project Manager as Agent." *The European Management Journal* 22, no 3: 327–336.

Wateridge, J.H. 1995. "IT Projects: A Basis for Success." *International Journal of Project Management* 13, no 3: 169–172.

Westerveld, E., and D. Gaya-Walters. 2001. *Het Verbeteren van uw Projectorganisatie: Het Project Excellence Model in de Praktijk.* Dementen, NL: Kluwer.

Zaccaro, S.J., A.L. Rittman, and M.A. Marks. 2001. "Team Leadership." *Leadership Quarterly* 12, no 4: 451–483.

Bibliography

Levicki, C. 1998. *The Leadership Gene.* London, UK: Financial Times Pitman Publishing.

Osborn, R.N., J.G. Hunt, and L.R. Jauch. 2002. "Toward a contextual theory of leadership." *The Leadership Quarterly* 13, no 6: 797–837.